Making a
Rattan Bow

DEDICATION
For Susanne & Telli

Making a Rattan Bow

Linda Schilling & Michael Wlotzka

Schiffer Publishing Ltd

4880 Lower Valley Road • Atglen, PA 19310

CONTENTS

PREFACE

In this book we would like to present a few bow designs that can be made with an amazing material, rattan. Let your imagination run free! Due to its excellent elastic properties, rattan has proven itself to be extremely suitable for building bows.

Since quite a few work steps are the same for each of the several bow designs, we did not go into the same detail in all the chapters. If a step is described in detail in one of the chapters, it might be that we touch upon it more briefly in the other chapters. The detailed descriptions have been highlighted in the contents list.

Have fun with the book!

Please note: Wood and rattan are natural materials. Every piece of wood or rattan reacts individually and can break, despite careful selection and cautious treatment. Wood dust can cause allergies.

The tools shown here have to be used with the necessary attention to health and safety precautions, otherwise there is a risk of injury.

Make sure that appropriate measures to ensure health and safety precautions are observed. All due care and diligence must be observed at all times!

This book is sold for information purposes only. Any use of the information presented in this book is at your own risk and responsibility.

Limit of Liability/Disclaimer of Warranty: While the publisher and the authors have used their best efforts in preparing this book, they make no representations or warranties with respect to the accuracy or completeness of the contents of this book and specifically disclaim any implied warranties of merchantability or fitness of use for a particular purpose. Neither the authors nor the publisher shall be held liable or responsible to any person or entity with respect to any loss or incidental or consequential damages caused, or alleged to have been caused, directly or indirectly, by the information contained herein. No warranty may be created or extended by sales representatives or written sales materials. The advice and strategies contained herein may not be suitable for your situation. You should consult with a professional where appropriate.

INFORMATION ABOUT RATTAN

Rattan pole with and without skin

Node at the stem

Cross-section of rattan pole showing the structure of the vascular bundles

Unpeeled and peeled poles

Some common names of the material are rattan, manau, rotan, malacca cane, and Spanish cane.

Rattan belongs to the Palmae family and is a fast growing palm with numerous subspecies.

Unlike typical palm trees, most rattans are climbing plants. Their slender stems with spines or hooks cling to nearby trees and can reach lengths of more than 100 meters. Stem diameters vary from 5 to 80 mm. On the leaf sheaths rattan forms a kind of swelling referred to as knee or node.

Rattan is a very light material, consisting of a soft flexible core and a protective hard periphery. Usually, the cross section has a round shape. The diffusely distributed vascular bundles run parallel to each other, the density of vascular bundles being higher in the outer part than the inner. This structural density distribution leads to a steady increase of stability from the inner to the outer portions. As a result, the elastic properties are very good in the outer portions, whereas the soft core shows a good absorbing capacity for deformation caused by bending.

In other words, rattan is an excellent material for bow making. Owing to its elastic properties, the outer part (back of the bow) behaves favorably with respect to tensile strength. At the same time, the soft core (belly of the bow) is better able to resist compression forces. Rattan can easily be bent by applying steam or heat; and after cooling and drying it retains its new shape.

Most commonly, rattan is commercially offered as peeled poles, around 4 cm in diameter and 2 to 4 m long.

RATTAN SHORT BOW *with* RECURVES

Type: Recurve bow
Material: Rattan
Length: ca. 130 cm
Draw weight: 25 lbs at 28 inches draw length

The basic design used for this rattan recurve bow can be made quite easily.

For this bow, we cut a rattan pole of 4 cm in diameter lengthwise in two halves. The aim is to build a bow 130 cm in length with a draw weight of 25 lbs at 28 inches draw length.

With such a short length in combination with a draw length of 28 inches, the bow string tends to slip off the nocks when the bow is fully drawn. To make sure that the bow string sits tight in the nock grooves, we have bent the ends of the bow limbs outwards into recurves.

Two versions are presented: In the first version, the bow is bending through the handle, forming a perfect arc of a circle (full compass), whereas in the second version we glue on a riser to get a stiff handle section. The dimensions are the same for both versions.

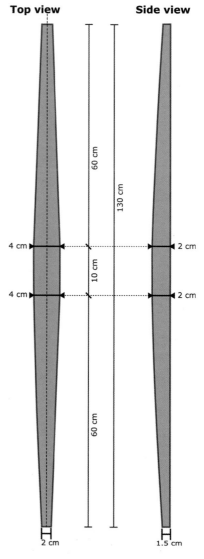

Top view · Side view
60 cm · 130 cm · 4 cm · 2 cm · 10 cm · 4 cm · 2 cm · 60 cm · 2 cm · 1.5 cm

Drawing the center line on the rattan pole fixed to a straight, squared timber

Sawing out the round rattan pole

Rattan pole cut into halves

1. Dimensions and Sawing-Out the Bow Profile

The total length of the bow stave, before bending the recurves, is about 130 cm. Over its total length, the 10 cm handle section is about 2 cm thick and 4 cm wide.

The top view profile is pyramid-shaped, meaning that the bow limbs are evenly tapered from the end of the handle area up to the ends of the bow. In our case that is from 4 cm to 2 cm in width (top view) and from 2 cm to 1.5 cm in thickness (side view).

Our rattan pole is about 4 cm in diameter, 2 m long, and looks more or less straight, but on second sight it is slightly twisted along its growth direction.

Before cutting the pole in two equal halves, we attach it to a plane squared timber and fixate it with duct tape. In this way we straighten out the slightly twisted pole and have a kind of "guiding device" for sawing out the round pole.

Then we draw a center line on the rattan pole, and along this center line saw it into halves. The square timber helps with the steering and prevents the round pole from turning around.

In order to outline the dimensions on one of the rattan halves, we put it on our workbench, the round part for the back of the bow facing down and the flat part for the belly facing up.

Since the rattan stave shows a slight twisting, it is necessary to first determine the correct center line. We stretch a string lengthwise over the stave and center it as much as possible. As a result, we can see that over a large part of the stave the string runs through the middle, but especially at the ends it shifts to the sides.

Rattan half with
centered string

Now, before cutting the 2 m long rattan pole to the projected length of 130 cm, we want to select the straightest part where the string runs nicely through the middle.

For this we need to mark the center line that will be the basis for drawing the top view.

We secure the string with some heavy objects and make sure it still runs as much as possible through the middle. Then we mark the spots where the string rests at each end of the stave. Using a long and straight metal slat, we now draw a line from one spot to the other to get our center line. We adjust the metal slat to the marked spots at each end, secure it with a clamp against slipping out of position, and draw a connecting line.

Marking of string position at the ends of the stave

At the ends of the stave the line is off-center, but over a large part it runs straight and exactly through the middle. That is the part from which we want to select the suitable 130 cm for the length of the bow.

We carefully inspect the stave and mark the section where the connecting line runs straight through the middle, and at the same time the edges of the rattan half run parallel to this center line. Within this section we measure up the required 130 cm.

Rattan half with straight metal slat

2 m long
rattan stave
with marked
center line

Marked for cutting the bow length

Cut on the marks

Then we cut the rattan stave at the marked points to the projected length.

Please note: If the rattan stave is heavily twisted, we might not be able to find a long enough straight section. In this case we have to straighten the rattan stave out a little by bending it over steam. In order to identify the twisted part, we look along the edges of the rattan half and mark the section that needs bending. Then we hold the marked part over a pot of boiling water for about 5 minutes. By then the rattan has become soft enough and we can bend it in the respective direction. After bending, we look along the edges again to check the result.

Well, now we have a straight stave of 130 cm in length and can start to draw the top view.

At first we need to outline the handle area - 10 cm in length and 4 cm in width over its total length. At 65 cm we make a mark for the bow's middle (width-wise), measure 5 cm to the left and 5 cm to the right, and mark the handle area.

From the ends of the handle area up to the tips we want the bow to taper off in width from 4 cm to 2 cm. For this, we go to the tips and make marks 1 cm to each side of the center line. Then we connect the marks at the tips with the marks at the end of the handle area.

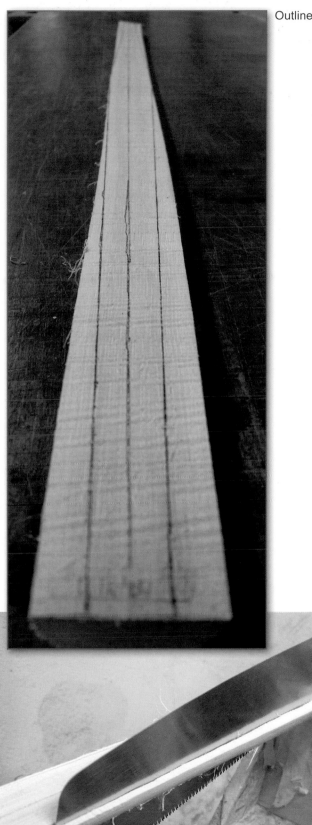
Outlined top view profile

Now the profile of the top view is outlined and we can cut out the contours. With a Japanese handsaw we cut exactly along the pencil lines to achieve an as much as possible straight edge.

Cutting out the top view

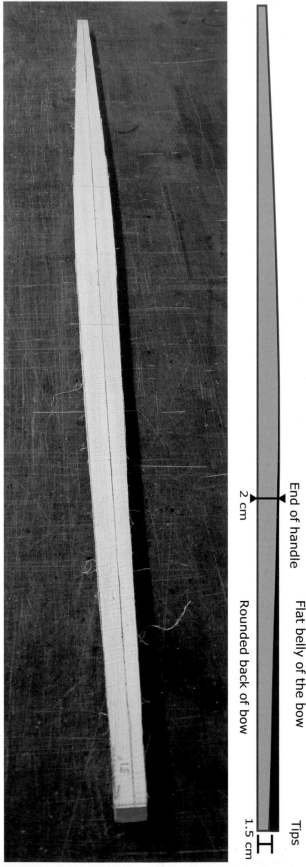

Top view of cut-out stave

2 cm

End of handle

Flat belly of the bow

Rounded back of bow

1.5 cm

Tips

Side view: Connecting line
between end of handle and
marking for the thickness

2. Preparing the Side Profile

In the top view the stave now tapers off from the handle area up to the tips, but it is still 2 cm thick over its total length (side view).

In order for the bow limbs to bend evenly, it is necessary to also taper the stave in thickness. Since we want the handle area to remain 2 cm thick, we extend the markings for the handle area over the edges on both sides of the stave. Just to be on the safe side we check again. The distance from each tip to the handle area is 60 cm and the length of the handle area is 10 cm.

For tapering down the limbs to a thickness of 1.50 cm at the tips, we have to take off material from the flat belly, because the rounded back has to remain untouched. Accordingly, we measure up 1.50 cm at the tips and connect the marking at the tips with the end of the handle area.

Then we repeat these steps for each side of each limb.

Using a saw for cutting out the contours could lead to unwelcome irregularities or distortions. In order to avoid that we are going to use a rasp to carefully reduce the thickness of the side profile.

The thickness should taper evenly from the ends of the handle area down to the tips. To facilitate things we add inclined facets on both sides of each limb.

Bow stave with side facets

Bow stave tapered to marked thickness

These facets make it easier to achieve an even taper and minimize the risk that we remove too much material and end up with hinges.

Since the limb has to be tapered down to the connecting line, this is also the baseline for the side facet. We have to take care that it remains intact when we work on the side facet. The side facet runs from the end of the handle area and gets broader towards the tips. In the middle we leave a middle facet, where we then carefully rasp the belly down to the marked thickness.

Now the side profile is prepared, with the surface of the belly being plane and even and the thickness of the stave tapering smoothly from the handle towards the tips.

This means that we have already created the best conditions to achieve an even bending of the limbs: both limbs taper evenly in width (top view) and in thickness (side view).

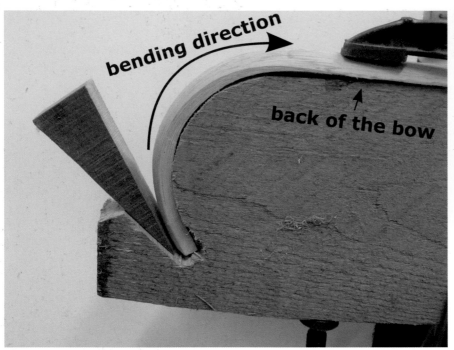

Bending of the recurves

Bow end secured with wedge

3. Bending the Recurves

When the bow is fully drawn, the short length of the bow leads to an unfavorable angle between bow string and tips. In order to prevent the bow string from slipping out, our bow gets so-called recurves, meaning it will be slightly bent outwards at the ends of the limbs.

We use a wooden form for bending the recurves. At first, we hold the end of the limb for about ten minutes over the steam of a pot with boiling water to make the rattan flexible. The following steps have to be carried out quite speedily. If the rattan cools down too much before we start bending, it might split. We put the bow end into the prepared form, with the back of the bow facing downwards, and secure it with a wedge. Then we carefully bend the stave over the form and fasten it with a clamp.

After the bow ends have cooled down for about ten minutes, we remove the stave from the form. We look along the sides of the bow and check the result. It might be that during bending the recurves have slightly twisted lengthwise.

If this is the case, we gently bend the still flexible recurves sideways to the left or to the right, until the bow stave looks straight again. In doing so, we have to be very careful that we do not accidentally bend the recurves out of shape.

After bending the recurves at both limbs, we leave the bow stave to dry for about two days. It is essential that the rattan dries long enough, because otherwise the recurves will not keep their shape.

Filing the
nock grooves

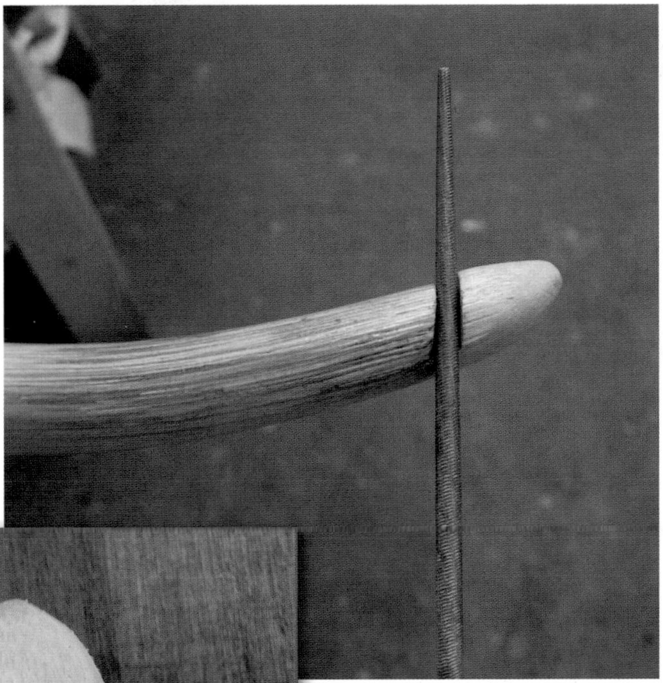

4. The Tillering

Before we can put the bow stave on
the tillering stick, we need to make
the nock grooves for holding the
bow string.

About 2 cm away from the tips,
using a round file, we file a 4 mm
deep, almost vertical groove into
one side of the limb and round it in
a slightly slanting angle towards
the belly of the bow. At the same
level we file in a groove at the
opposite side. Here it is important
to make sure that there remains a
sufficiently large space between the
grooves and that the grooves are
symmetrical and do not have any
sharp edges.

Nock groove
on the belly
of the bow

Nock groove on back of the bow

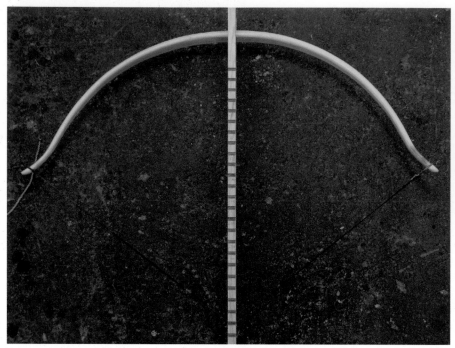

Bow at 28 inches (full draw) bending through the handle

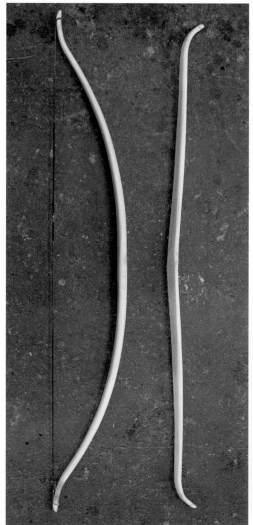

Rattan recurve in strung and in unstrung condition

After having filed the nock grooves into both limbs, we put the bow string on the bow and place it on the tillering stick. Because of the elastic properties of rattan and the even taper of the limbs achieved by careful preparation of top and side profile, the bow can be drawn considerably already. But, it is also true for rattan: don't overdraw the bow! Rather draw a little bit less in the beginning than too much.

We step back a bit from the tillering stick and check the tiller. The limbs are bending quite nicely. So the next step will be to tiller the bow as described on pages 74 and 75, until the bow is bending evenly over its total length and we have reached the intended draw length.

5. Handle Variations

Version A: The bow bends through the handle and will get a wrapping of buffalo leather lace. For this version it is not necessary to make any changes in the handle area. During tillering we have ensured that there is a homogenous transition from the handle to the limbs, so that the handle is bending when the bow is drawn.

At first we sand and wax the surface of the bow. As a result, all previous markings have been removed from the bow. This means we have to measure the bow middle again, before we start wrapping brown leather lace around the handle. As an optical accentuation we are going to apply a strip of black fabric at the ends of the wrapping.

Wrapping leather lace around the bow handle

For fixation we place the beginning of the lace under the wrapping.

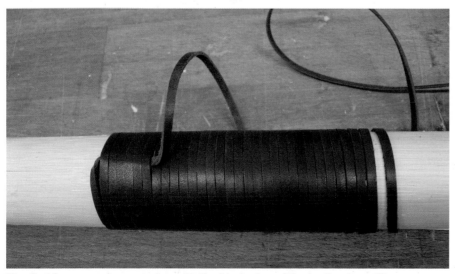

The first few wrappings overlap with the beginning of the leather lace. The excess gets cut off later.

Also at the other end we place the leather lace under the wrapping

Then we pull the leather lace tight around the handle.

Version A: Flat handle wrapped with a buffalo leather lace

Version A: Braced bow with "full compass" and leather wrapping

About 6 cm from the middle of the bow we wrap a 2 cm broad strip of black fabric around the handle and fix the ends with a drop of glue.

For a seamless transition, we put the leather lace on top of the black strip and start wrapping it around the whole handle area. We have to apply quite a bit of tension to pull the leather lace tight. This is important for the tightness of the overlappings at the ends of the wrapping.

Version B:
Bow and
piece of
rattan to be
glued onto
the handle.

Version B: The bow gets a glued-on handle piece. As a result, the bow will not bend in the handle area anymore, but have a stiff handle.

The other half of the rattan pole is left over from cutting the profile. From this we choose an about 14 cm long and straight piece to glue onto the handle.

The gluing has to be done before sanding the surface of the bow. The surfaces to be glued together need to be clean, dust free, and fat-free.

Bow and handle piece clamped together.

Handle piece before gluing

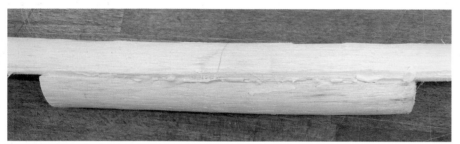

Handle piece after gluing

After thorough clean up with a clean brush, we apply glue onto both surfaces - following the manufacturer's instructions. Then we align the two pieces and clamp them together, as firmly as possible, so that a small amount of glue squeezes out of the sides.

According to the manufacturer's instructions on compression time, we allow the glue to cure before we take off the clamps.

After the glue has cured well (see manufacturer's instructions), we can start to shape the handle.

With a coarse rasp, we level off the edges of the handle piece. In order to achieve a smooth transition from the handle into the limbs we work carefully from the end of the handle to the middle. Working the other way round increases the risk of moving the rasp too far and taking off too much material, which would then result in hinges in the limbs.

Shaping the handle with a rasp

The rounded handle fades smoothly into the limbs

Braced bow with stiff handle

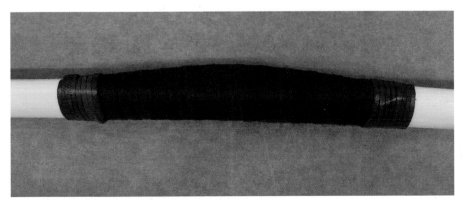

Wrapping the handle with textile adhesive tape

When the transitions from the handle to the limbs are smooth and the handle is rounded nicely, we grind the surface smooth with sandpaper and give the bow a protective coating of wax, pure linseed oil or tung oil.

Since it can take a few weeks before oils have completely cured, we prefer to use wood wax, which gives the surface a velvet-like shine and brings out the texture of the material.

Since we want to use textile adhesive tape for the wrapping of the handle that would not adhere to a waxed or oiled surface, we spare out the handle area from coating.

We wrap the adhesive tape tight around the whole handle area. To avoid gaps we overlap the strips a little bit and press them on carefully.

Finally, we wrap brown buffalo leather lace around the ends of the textile wrapping. This protects the edges of the textile tape from fraying and at the same time forms a nice contrast.

Wrapping with leather lace at the end

And this is how our finished bow looks:

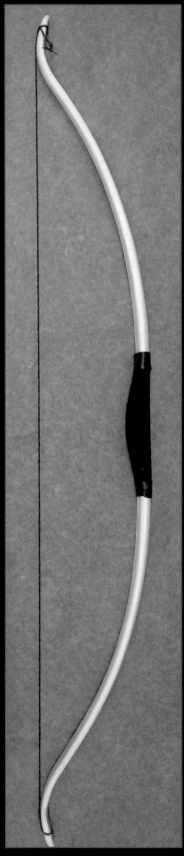

Rattan recurve, 25 lbs at 28 inches, length 130 cm

Unbraced bow with glued-on handle

Braced bow with stiff handle and leather wrapping

Wrapping of brown buffalo leather lace with black textile border

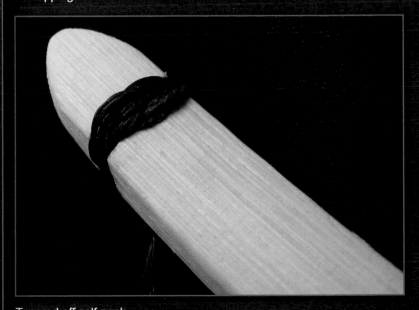

Tapered off self nock

Side view

Top view

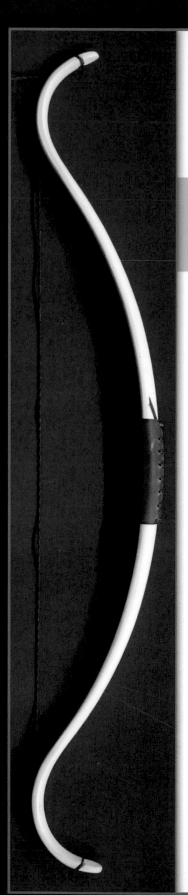

RATTAN SHORT BOW
with RECURVES *and* ROSEWOOD BELLY

Type: Recurve bow
Material: Rattan, Rosewood
Length: approx. 110 cm
Draw weight: 40 lbs at 28 inches draw length

In this design the bow bends through the handle (full compass), meaning the bow has a circular tiller and bends evenly over its entire length, bringing out the full potential of the rattan.

Due to the unfavorable string angle at the nocks resulting from the short bow length of 110 cm, the bow string tends to dislodge when the bow is drawn. To prevent the bow string from slipping, this short bow will get pronounced recurves and a string groove on the belly side to support the bow string.

To achieve an increase in draw weight and to strengthen the compression zone of the bow, we will glue a 5 mm thick piece of rosewood veneer to the belly.

This chapter also deals in detail with the dimensions and the lacing of the leather handle.

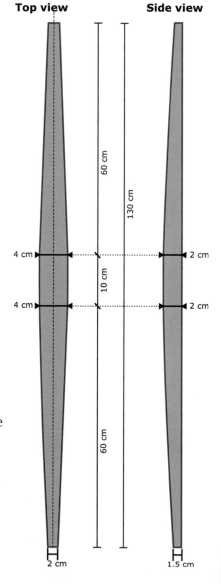

Rattan short bow with recurves and glued-on rosewood veneer on the belly of the bow, 40 lbs at 28 inches, length 110 cm

Cutting the rattan pole into halves

1. Preparing the Bow Stave

For the dimensions, we use the same profile as for the recurve bow on page 8.

This means we start from a length of 130 cm. Then, after bending the recurves, the total length will come out at about 110 cm.

In the top view, the bow is about 10 cm long and 4 cm wide in the handle area and then tapers down to 2 cm at the tips. In the side view, the bow tapers down from 2 cm at the handle to 1.5 cm at the tips.

To find more details, see pages 9 and 10 on.

At first, we cut the rattan pole (diameter 4 cm) lengthwise in the middle. With the help of a string we determine the longitudinal middle of the bow and mark the center line.

In terms of the length of the bow, we select the straightest section of the rattan halves and mark the middle for the handle. From there, we measure 65 cm to the left and 65 cm to the right for the lengths of the limbs and cut the rattan half down to the intended length of 130 cm.

For the handle area, we measure up 5 cm from the middle to each side and mark it.

Drawing the center line

Marked center line

Outlining the
top view of
the bow

At each end of the stave we measure out from the center line 1 cm to the left and 1 cm to the right (2 cm width at the tips).

Then we draw connecting lines between the markings at the tips and the respective markings at the ends of the handle area.

Along these lines we saw out the top view profile of the stave as precisely as possible.

After we have done so for both limbs, we are going to adjust the side profile.

The handle area is already 2 cm thick, as required (half the diameter of the rattan pole). We want the limbs to taper evenly from the handle up to the tips. So from the round back of the bow we measure up 1.5 cm at the sides of the tips and draw a straight line to the ends of the handle.

Then we saw out the side profile as precisely as possible along these connecting lines, or we use a rasp to carefully taper down the thickness (see pages 14 and 15.)

Now our stave shows an even taper from the ends of the handle to the tips, in the top view and in the side view.

Before gluing the rosewood veneer on the belly of the bow, the next step will be to prepare the surfaces to be glued and bend the recurves into the limbs.

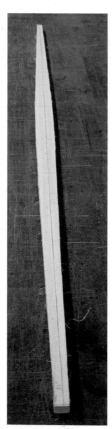

Top view of
sawn-out stave

Side view of sawn-out stave

Roughening the belly with a tooth plane

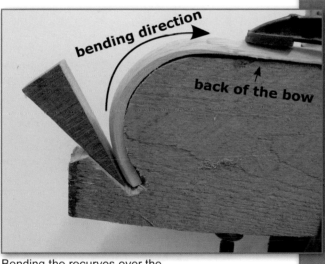

bending direction

back of the bow

Bending the recurves over the prepared wooden form

Bow stave with
steam-bent
recurves

Before we can bend the recurves, we have to prepare the surfaces for gluing. With a tooth plane we roughen the surface of the rattan belly. The resulting fine scratches enlarge the surface which adds to a better adhesion of the glue.

Analogously, we also roughen the corresponding surface of the rosewood veneer.

Beforehand, we have built a wooden form with the intended bending radius for the recurves. To make the rattan easy to bend, it has to be heated. But, since heating has a negative effect on the adhesive bond, it is necessary to shape the recurves before we do the gluing.

The bending of the recurves is explained in more detail from page 16 on.

At first, we steam the ends of the bow for about 10 minutes over a pot with boiling water. As soon as the rattan has become flexible enough, we put the bow end into the form, fix it with a wedge, bend the recurves around the wooden form and fasten the limb with a clamp. Here it is essential that we work speedily and pay attention to the correct bending direction.

After that, we leave the rattan to cool off sufficiently and then repeat the same procedure for the other limb.

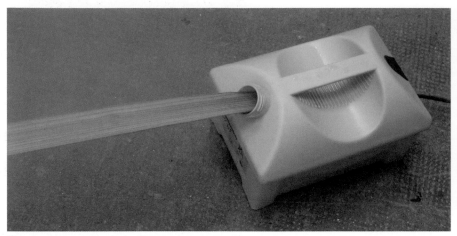

Heating the veneer in boiling water

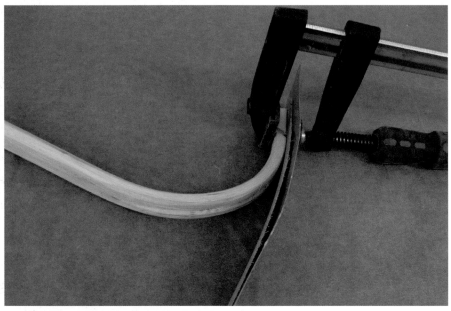

Bending the veneer: applying the first clamp

Veneer fastened with clamps

Next are the recurves for the rosewood veneer. Here, too, it is necessary to bend the recurves before gluing, because otherwise the veneer might collapse when it gets bent over the rattan recurves.

In order to have some leeway for later corrections, the veneer is about 2 cm longer and wider than the bow stave.

We start with heating the rosewood veneer for about 10 minutes in boiling water.

The next steps have to be done quickly, because the veneer cools off quite fast and then loses its flexibility.

That is why we have put within reach all the things we will need: our bow stave, a few clamps and a thin metal slat. The metal band, as an intermediate layer between the veneer and the clamps, will avoid pressure marks and make sure that no wood fibers come off when bending the veneer.

After heating, we instantly lay the veneer and the metal slat on the belly of the bow and attach the first clamp exactly at the end of the bow. Then we very carefully bend the veneer and the metal band over the recurves of the bow stave and fasten both with additional clamps.

Bow stave and veneer with recurves

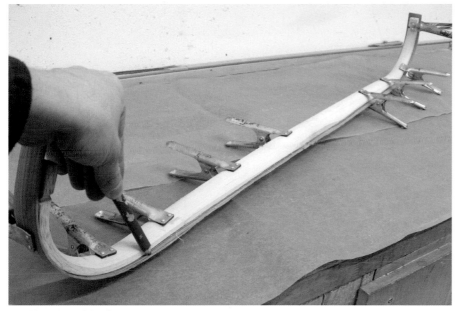
Marking the width flush to the stave

Trimming the veneer to the width of the bow stave

Now we have to wait for about half an hour, until the material has cooled off well. Then we can remove the clamps.

At the other end we bend the veneer in basically the same way, but keep in mind that both recurves and the length of the veneer have to match. Consequently, we have to align all three layers properly before we start bending the veneer over the recurves of the rattan stave.

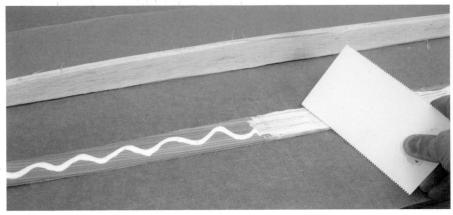

Applying the glue with a notched trowel

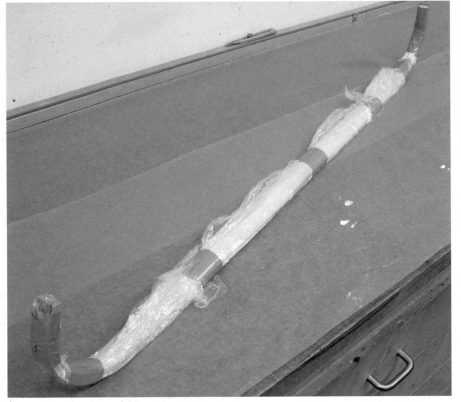

Bow stave and veneer—wrapped with plastic wrap and fastened with duct tape

Bow stave lying on its side, recurves with clamps supported by pieces of wood

Before gluing we have to trim off the excess veneer from around the edges.

With the veneer being flush to the bow stave, we make sure that both pieces can be put together properly and do not get out of place during gluing.

We place the rosewood veneer in such a position that it fits smoothly and as tension-free as possible to the belly of the bow, and fasten it with spring clamps. With a pencil we mark the excess and saw it off along the marking lines.

Important: for gluing, read manufacturer's instructions and strictly follow safety recommendations on glue and solvents!

See a more detailed description on gluing from page 42 on.

After thorough cleaning and degreasing of the bonding surfaces, we spread appropriate glue evenly over the surfaces to be glued together.

After that, we press the bonding surfaces firmly together, so that the edges are flush. Then we wrap plastic wrap around bow stave and veneer, making sure that no plastic wrap gets between the bonding surfaces. The plastic wrap prevents the glue from sticking to the clamps or the working surfaces.

We carefully secure our package with tape, so that the veneer will not get out of place when we attach the clamps. Especially in the section of the recurves, we take care that the fastening is sufficiently strong.

The recurves will be heavily loaded by the weight of the clamps. To prevent them from twisting under the load, we lay the bow stave on its side and support the recurves by putting suitable pieces of wood underneath. Then we can start to set the clamps.

Rounding the edges of the veneer

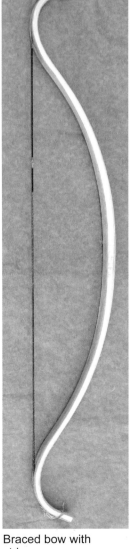

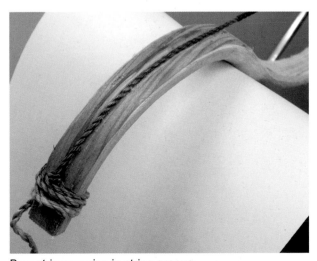

Filing a string groove into the recurves

Bow string running in string groove

Braced bow with string groove

At the end of the compression time, as recommended by the manufacturer, we remove the clamps and the plastic wrap to allow the glue to completely dry in the air.

Only after complete curing can we continue to work on our bow. We start with removing all residual glue and then round the edges of the veneer evenly along the belly of the bow.

As described in further detail from page 17 on, we file two symmetric nock grooves in both sides of the tips. Because of the extreme bending at the recurve ends, we work a string groove into the recurves (see a more detailed description from page 103 on).

Now our bow is ready for being braced with the bow string for the first time, and then we can start with tillering.

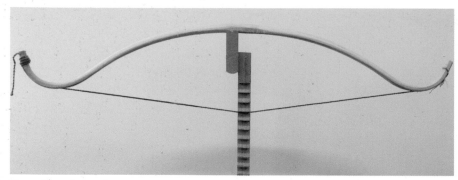

Bow at low brace

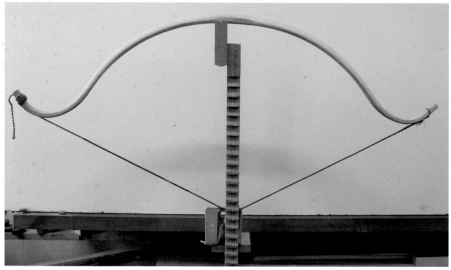

After each tillering step the bow gets drawn a little bit further,so that the impact of the removal can take effect

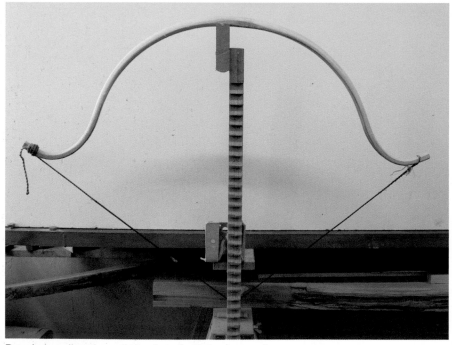

Bow is bending through the handle (full compass)

2. Tillering the Bow

The basic principle of tillering is described in more detail from page 74 on. However, this bow is kind of a special case. Since the veneer that we have glued onto the belly of the bow is relatively thin, there is hardly any margin left for removing material.

Removing too much material might result in large sections being rasped down to the rattan surface, or the veneer might get so thin that it collapses when pressure is applied. This is the reason why we take off material primarily from the edges of the belly.

First of all, we find and mark the sections of the limbs that are too stiff. In these too stiff sections we rasp off only very small amounts directly from the belly. Instead, we taper the edges of the veneer into fine inclined facets and round them down so that they harmoniously blend into the limbs.

The recurve ends are not supposed to bend and will remain stiff. But, because we want the short bow to be bending through the handle, we also tiller the section of the handle area until we have achieved an even bending over the total length of the bow.

After each tillering step we pull the bow string a little bit further down on the tillering stick and check the result. It is only through additional stress (further bending of the bow) that the removal of material makes an impact.

When we continue with the tillering, we try to avoid removing any more wood from the belly of the bow, but concentrate on the edges. But also there we cannot take off an unlimited amount, otherwise the limbs will become too slim or disharmonious in shape.

After a few more tillering steps we have already removed quite a lot of material from the sides, without having achieved the desired bending, but don't want to make the limbs any narrower. In this case we, can take off material from the back of the bow. We mark the too-stiff sections on the back of the bow where we evenly sand off a fine layer of the rattan.

Done! Our bow is now tillered to the desired draw weight and shows an even bending of the handle area, as well as the limbs. Now it is time to test-shoot our bow and make a final check on the tillering stick.

After sanding off all tool marks and scratches with 120, 240 and 400 grit sanding paper, we apply wood wax to the surface with a brush. In the handle area we protect the surface with a piece of adhesive tape, because there we want to fix the leather grip with a drop of glue later. Finally, we polish the surface with a sheet of paper, until our bow gets a nice shine.

Removing scratches and tool marks with sand paper

Applying wood wax with a brush

Polishing of waxed surface with a sheet of paper

For shaping, the leather piece is clamped around the handle area.

Imprints of the spring clamps on the piece of leather

Cutting the edge at a distance of 5 mm to the imprints

Marking auxiliary points for the grip holes

3. Leather Grip

At last, we want to make a laced leather grip for our bow. For the leather grip, we have chosen a piece of pit-tanned sleek leather, about 1.5 mm thick and cut to the dimensions of 13 cm to 13 cm.

We soak the leather in water for about five minutes to make it smooth and easier to shape. Then we let it dry for a while until it is not dripping wet anymore, but only damp. Damp leather is soft and elastic, and easy to work on.

When we put the leather piece around the handle, we make sure to place the slack sides for the lacing on the back of the bow. Then we pull the leather tight around the handle and attach the spring clamps.

Shortly afterwards, we take off the spring clamps and take a look at the leather piece. The spring clamps have left imprints on the leather which will serve as a reference for the cutting of the leather.

During drying the leather will shrink a little bit. This we have to consider when cutting the edges and punching the holes.

For this reason we do not shorten the leather directly along the imprints, but place our ruler at a distance of 5 mm from the imprints. With a sharp knife we cut off the overhanging leather in a straight line.

After we have trimmed both sides of the leather, we pierce small auxiliary points for the eight grip holes into the leather, at a distance of about 1 cm to the edges. We start with piercing the first and the last holes about 5 mm from each edge, then placing the other auxiliary points at equal intervals in-between.

Punching the holes for the lacing

For the lacing, we have chosen an approximately 3 mm wide lace of buffalo leather. To make sure that the leather lace can be pulled easily through the grip holes, these should have a slightly bigger diameter of approximately 3.5 mm.

With a hole punch, we punch the grip holes centrally over the marked auxiliary points on both sides of the leather grip.

To prevent the leather grip from turning out of position later, we want to fix it with a drop of glue. During waxing we had attached a piece of adhesive tape to the belly of the bow to keep part of the handle area free from grease. Now we remove the tape and apply a drop of glue.

Then we turn the bow over, position the piece of leather around the middle of the handle and immediately start to pull the lace through the grip holes.

Fixing the leather grip with a drop of glue

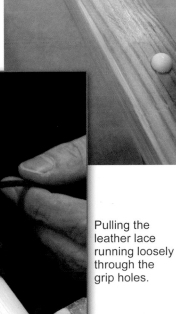

Pulling the leather lace running loosely through the grip holes.

Leather
lace running
loosely
through the
grip holes

For this lacing technique we place the leather lace straight over the upside of the leather piece and pull it through the grip holes that are on the same level. On the underside the lace is run diagonally to the following pair of holes and pulled through from below. Then again straight over the upside and so on, we pull the lace loosely through all the grip holes.

Tightening the
leather lace

Pulling
the lacing
tight with a
teaspoon
handle

Fastening
the ends
with a knot

After having threaded the leather lace through all the holes, we tighten the lace until the leather grip fits tightly around the handle. With the help of a teaspoon handle, we pull the parallel lacings one after the other really tight, and fasten the ends of the lace with a knot.

Bow grip of pit-tanned leather with buffalo leather lacing

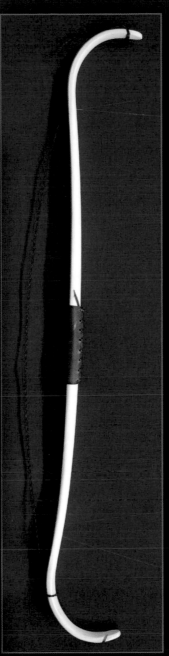

Side view of rattan short bow with recurves

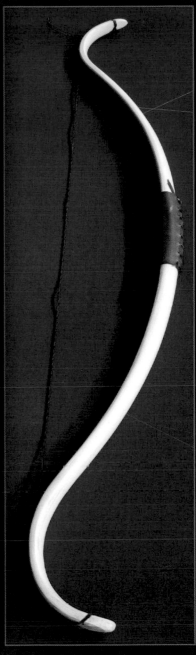

Rattan short bow with recurves and backing of veneer on the belly, 40 lbs at 28 inches, length 110 cm

Pronounced recurves with string groove

Backing of veneer on the belly of the bow

PYRAMID BOW *of* ASH WOOD *with* RATTAN BACKING

Type: Pyramid Bow
Material: Ash wood and Rattan
Length: ca. 165 cm
Draw weight: 55 lbs at 28 inches

For this pyramid style bow we have used ash wood for the belly of the bow and rattan as backing for the back of the bow. The nock overlays are made of steamed pearwood. The handle area is wrapped with brown buffalo leather lace. With a length of approximately 165 cm the target is to achieve a draw weight of over 50 lbs at a draw length of 28 inches.

Rattan for the back of bow: During bending the back of the bow is exposed to tension forces. Because of its elastic properties rattan is particularly suitable to absorb these tension forces.

Ash tree for the belly of the bow: During bending the belly of the bow is more exposed to compression forces. For our bow we have chosen compact ash wood for the belly.

These two parts of different materials have been glued together with a glue that is suitable for permanent and water-tight connections of wood.

For the belly of the bow we choose a dressed plank or board of ash wood, taking great care that the wood grain in longitudinal direction runs in as much as possible straight and parallel lines and that there are no knots in the section for the bow stave.

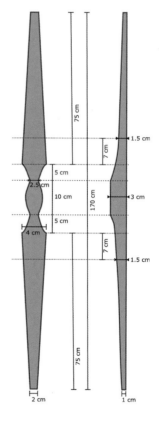

Pyramid bow of ash wood with a backing of rattan

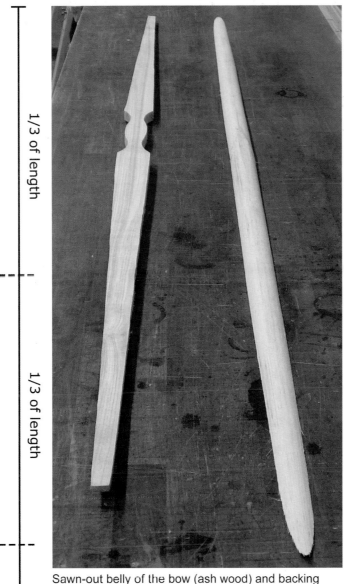

1/3 of length

1/3 of length

2 cm

1/3 of length

1 cm

Sawn-out belly of the bow (ash wood) and backing
(rattan)

Half-round outside part
of the rattan backing with
parallel fiber course (see
picture at right) remains
untouched. Inner cut surface
will be tapered.

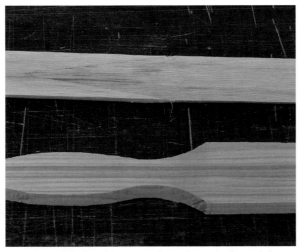

Top view of belly of bow, cut into shape before gluing.
Rattan backing retains whole width until after gluing.

1. Top View

First of all, we identify the section
of the board where we want to
outline the top view of the bow.
This section has to be free of knots
and, of course, we choose the part
of the board where the wood grain
runs nice and straight. In this
section we are going to lay out the
dimensions and then saw out the
top view. At the ends we will leave
a margin of a few centimeters,
which will give us some flexibility
later, for the gluing.

With the side profile we will
deal later, after we have glued on
the rattan backing.

2. Backing of Rattan

For the backing of rattan we cut
the rattan pole (diameter 4 cm) to
the projected length and then in
symmetrical halves. On each
outward end (1/3 of length) we
taper the surface down to a
thickness of 1 cm at the tips
(compare page 14). We prefer to
use a rasp in doing so, but a draw
knife or a plane will also do the
job.

For the gluing operation, we will
retain the whole width of the
rattan backing. Only after the
backing and belly of the bow have
been glued together, will we cut
out the top view.

Plane with toothed blade cuts fine grooves into the surface.

When attaching the clamps some glue should squeeze out of the joint.

3. Gluing Belly of the Bow and Backing Together

Before gluing, each bonding surface has to be prepared in order to achieve the best possible adhesion.

The stability of adhesive bonds largely depends on the size of the adhesive surfaces. The visible surfaces of our bow parts look relatively smooth. Therefore, we will roughen the bonding surfaces in order to increase their size. For this we use a plane with a toothed blade that cuts fine grooves into the surface. Alternatively, we sand the surface with coarse sandpaper.

In order to achieve a good adhesion, it is essential to obtain a close contact between the surface of the workpiece and the glue. This is why the bonding surfaces have to be clean, dust-free and fat-free.

First, we remove the coarse dust particles resulting from the roughening of the surface. With a brush or paintbrush we carefully brush down the surfaces.

Caution: Wear an appropriate respirator! Wood dust can be toxic and cause allergic reactions.

But we are not finished yet. Apart from the visible particles there is also grease from our fingers, abrasive dust from sanding or planing, or the like that have to be removed from the surfaces, too. For this we use acetone.

Caution: Observe all safety instructions and danger warnings on the container! Acetone is highly flammable and can be dangerous to your health! Always take appropriate safety precautions! Wear appropriate respirator, gloves and face protection! Do not use in closed rooms!

At first, we clear some space on our workbench and cover it with non-stick baking paper, so that after degreasing the bow parts we can put them in a clean place and at the same time have an underlay for when we do the gluing. Wearing face protection, respirator and appropriate disposable gloves, we thoroughly brush down the bonding surfaces with a scrubbing brush and acetone. Then we wait for a little while to be sure that the acetone has completely evaporated.

Now the belly of the bow and the backing are ready for gluing. We use a two-component glue specially designed for adhesive connections subjected to high stress.

Caution: Wear protective gloves!

Following the manufacturer's instructions, we mix the two components and apply the glue evenly across the whole area of the bonding surfaces.

While we leave the rattan backing lying on the workbench with the bonding surface facing up, we position the belly and press the bonding surfaces together. We make sure that both parts lie perfectly on top of each other and do not slip sideways or lengthwise out of position. When both parts are placed straight on top of each other, we start to attach the clamps.

The first clamp will be attached in the middle of the bow. From there we place the following clamps at intervals of approximately 10 cm up to the ends of the limbs, making sure that both bow parts are pressed together firmly, but do not slip out of position when tightening the clamps.

Leaving the rattan backing a little bit longer makes it easier to position the pieces during gluing

Make sure to have enough clamps before you start with the gluing.

Cutting the bow stave with a hand saw

Bow ends cut flush. At the top, rattan backing. At the bottom, belly of the bow from ashwood. Please note the excess rattan on the right and left.

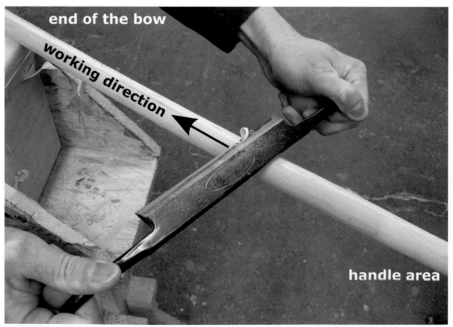

end of the bow

working direction

handle area

With the draw knife the working direction is from the handle area to the ends of the bow. Using the draw knife against the working direction may lead to chipping in the rattan.

Information about compression and drying times can be found in the manufacturer's instructions. After the recommended compression time has expired, we remove the clamps and check the result. Both parts of our bow stave stick together well and nothing got out of place. However, before we can continue to work on our stave, the glue needs to be completely cured. The drying time of glue depends on many factors, such as temperature and air humidity.

When the glue has fully dried, we have to adjust the rattan backing to the top view of the belly and cut the side view into shape before we can start with the tillering process.

4. Preparing the Laminated Bow Stave for Tillering

At both ends of our bow stave we cut the ends flush with each other, depending on how much margin we had left earlier when cutting out the profile.

As can be seen in the photo at left, the rattan backing is protruding over the sides and has to be adjusted to the top view of the belly. For this we place our bow stave in the vice with one of the sides facing upwards, so that we can easily remove the excess with a draw knife.

Worked out edges at the handle

Working off the edges on the left and on the right of the handle. With the draw knife it is easy to quickly remove big amounts of wood.

Rounding the edges of the handle with a rasp

After we have removed the excess material on each side of the bow stave with the draw knife, we also have to take off the protruding rattan in the handle area. For this we use a rasp, because with a rasp it is easier to work on round edges.

Having removed all the excess in the handle area and at the limbs, the rattan backing and the belly are flush to one another now (top view). What we still need to do is prepare the side view: We draw the dimensions on our bow stave and cut out the side profile.

The next step is to prepare the belly of the bow. Starting with the handle, we use a draw knife or a rasp to work off the edges on the right and on the left side of the handle area, thus creating three facets: a plane one in the middle and inclined ones on each side.

After that, we give final shape to the handle by rounding the edges with a rasp, until the handle is nice and round and fits well in the hand.

After having formed the handle, we will now attend to the shape of the limbs. On the belly we carefully round down the edges on the left and on the right of the limbs with a rasp, making sure that we get a floating and even curvature from the handle up to the ends of the bow.

We run the rasp with long movements along the limbs to ensure an even removal of wood. Choppy or short movements with the rasp may result in taking off too much wood from some areas and then having to deal with unwelcome hinges in the limbs during tillering.

The amount of wood we remove from the sides of the limbs has, of course, already an impact on the targeted draw weight. The more we rasp off, the more decreases the draw weight. Therefore, we try to take off as little as possible wood for now. If necessary, we can

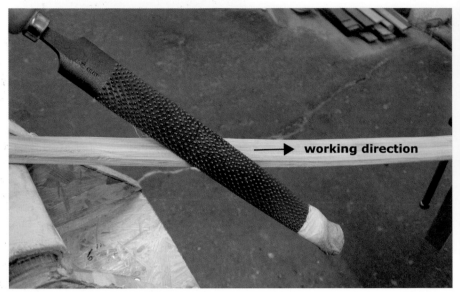

working direction

When rounding the edges, the rasp is run with long movements along the limb

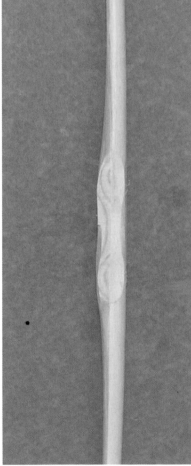

Rounded handle and sides of the limbs

reduce the draw weight later by removing wood again at the edges.

After we have rounded down each side of both limbs, our bow stave is ready for tillering. In the tillering process we want to achieve an even and uniform bending of both limbs of the bow.

5. Tillering

During the tillering process we will synchronize the limbs in such a way that they will be bending evenly and equally (compare page 74). We put our bow stave on the tillering stick - the center of the bow resting in the hollow on the top, and the rattan backing on the back of the bow facing upwards. For drawing the bow stave we use a bow stringer with leather caps that are slipped over the tips.

Now we can bend our bow for the first time. We cautiously pull the bow stringer down and place it in a notch of the tillering stick.

From a distance we examine the bending. All sections are supposed to bend evenly. The sections on the belly of the bow that are bending less than the adjacent sections are still too stiff, and we have to remove wood there to adjust the bending. We mark those stiff sections with the tiller tool or with a pencil. Then we take the bow stave off the tillering stick and cautiously rasp off wood from the spots that are too stiff.

After each tillering step the bow stave has to be stressed a bit more, so that the wood removal can take effect. In view of that, we put our stave back on the tillering stick, pull the bow stringer a bit further down and insert it in the next notch, thus increasing the bending of the bow.

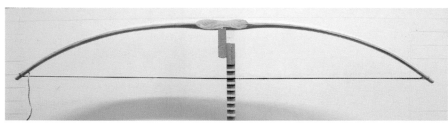

On the tillering stick we can check the bending of the limbs and the balance between the limbs.

Bow braced with bow string on the tillering stick

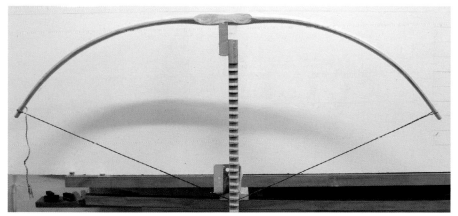

Braced bow on the tillering stick. Both limbs are bending evenly, in the handle area the bow remains stiff.

Again we mark the stiffer sections on the belly of the bow and remove some wood from there. We repeat this procedure several times until we have achieved an even bending.

For the next tillering steps we want to use a bow string to put up our bow on the tillering stick. So we need nock grooves at each end of the bow that will hold the bow string in place. With a round file (diameter 4 mm) we carve the nock grooves into both limbs, about 2 cm away from the tips.

Now we brace the bow with the bow string, center it loosely on the tillering stick and check the result.

When we now hook the bow string into a notch of the tillering stick, we have to keep in mind that the bow stringer is longer than the bow, whereas the bow string is shorter than the bow. For this reason we cannot place the bow string in the previous notch, but have to gently pull it downwards to find an appropriate notch further up without bending the bow too far.

Now we continue with the tillering process as before: We mark the stiff spots on the belly of the bow and remove wood there. After each tillering step we pull the bow string one notch further down until we have achieved the targeted draw length.

Now that we have achieved the desired draw length and both limbs are bending evenly, it is time to do the first test-shoots with our bow.

The outer edges of the limbs are not smooth enough yet, so we round them down just a little bit more with a fine file, but take care not to impair the bending by removing too much wood on one spot. In case the draw weight is still too high, we take off small amounts of wood evenly along the edges to weaken the limbs.

With a draw knife, we carefully flatten the round surface of the rattan backing at the tips.

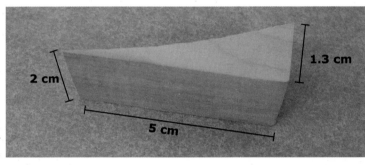

Dimensions of wedges for the overlays

2 cm

1.3 cm

5 cm

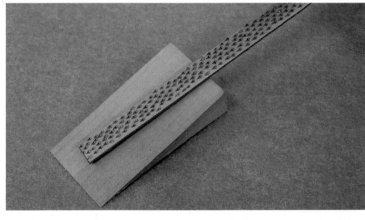

Roughening the bonding surfaces with a small rasp

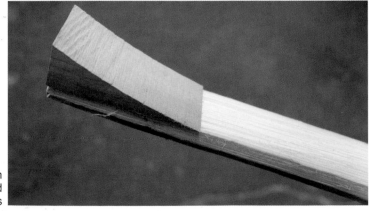

Glued-on pearwood overlays

6. Wood Overlays for the Tips

As a reinforcement and also for aesthetic reasons we want to attach overlays of pearwood onto the ends of the bow.

In order to get a plane bonding surface for the overlays, we have to flatten the half-round rattan backing at the tips.

Out of a piece of pearwood we cut two triangular wedges (length about 5 cm, width about 2 cm, and height about 1.3 cm). The long bottom side of the wedge will be glued on the rattan backing, so we make sure that this surface is plane and flat.

Before gluing, we have to roughen the bonding surfaces and clean them from dust and grease.

Then we apply an appropriate glue (e.g. two-component epoxy resin glue) evenly to the bonding surface at the tips and to the bonding surface of the overlay, position both pieces flush against each other and gently press them together.

Attention: Wear protective gloves!

To spare us the trouble of having to scrape off all the residual glue after it has dried, we now remove the glue that is squeezing out at the sides with a cloth, taking care that the overlays do not slip out of position.

Rounding off the sides of the overlays toward the middle, with a file.

Rounding off the bottom of the overlays to create a tip at the end of the bow

Sanding the round edges of the overlays

After the glue has cured completely, we are going to shape the overlays. To facilitate working on the sides of the bow, we place the bow stave sideways in the vise.

We file off the protruding parts of the pearwood until the overlays are flush against the rattan backing.

Then we round off the overlays from the sides towards the bow middle, making the two sides meet in the middle and form a tip at the end of the bow.

Finally, we round off the bottom of the overlays from the belly up to the tip, so that we obtain a smooth and even curvature.

The different layers of wood that join in the tips give a nice look to the bow.

After we have shaped the overlays for both limbs in this way, we sand the entire bow with sanding paper to get a smooth surface without tool marks.

Caution: Wear an appropriate respirator!

We start with 180-grit sanding paper, change then to 300-grit and finally to 500-grit sanding paper.

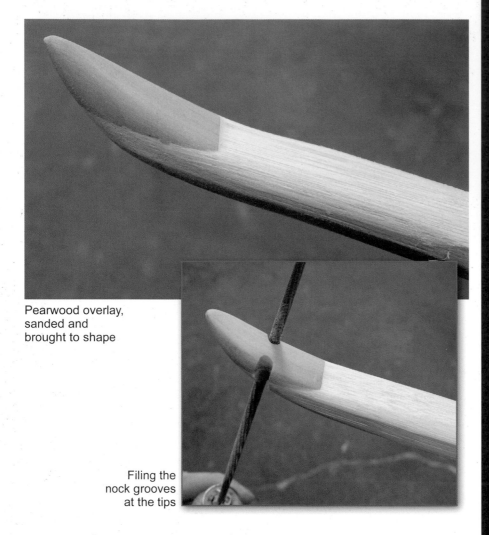

Pearwood overlay,
sanded and
brought to shape

Filing the
nock grooves
at the tips

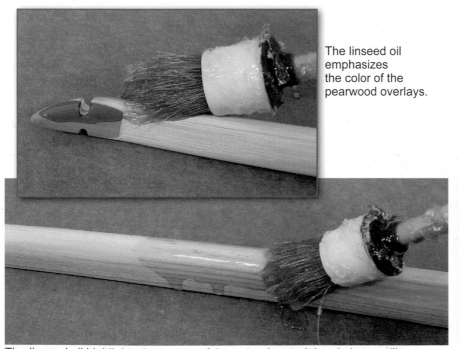

The linseed oil
emphasizes
the color of the
pearwood overlays.

The linseed oil highlights the texture of the natural material and gives a silky shine.

What is left to do is to carve the nock grooves into the pearwood overlays. Based on the already existing nock grooves in the belly of the bow and the backing, we use a round file to extend the nock grooves into the overlays. Here it is essential that the grooves are located at the same level on each side and are deep enough to hold the bow string safely in place.

Our bow is ready now for the finishing touches. For protection of the surface against damages and humidity we will apply pure linseed oil that, after curing, will leave a protective coat on the bow and at the same time emphasize the natural texture of the wood. Linseed oils with additives such as cooking oil cannot be used, because the additives prevent the oil from hardening.

We apply the linseed oil with a paintbrush evenly and not too thickly over the entire surface of the bow, let it soak in for a few minutes and then wipe off the excess oil with a cloth.

Caution: Cloth soaked with linseed oil is prone to spontaneous combustion and can ignite spontaneously. Never leave it unattended, let it dry spread-out on a non-flammable surface by exposure to air, soak it in water, or keep it in an air-tight container!

To ensure that the bow feels comfortable and smooth in the hand, we wrap 3mm wide lace of brown buffalo leather around the handle. The dark brown gives a nice contrast to the bright colors of the bow.

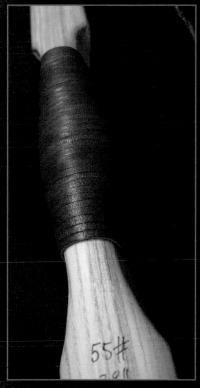

Handle wrapped with brown buffalo leather lace

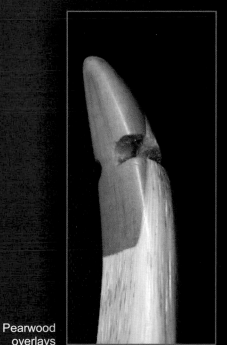

Pearwood overlays

Top view of pyramid shape

Unbraced pyramid bow, little set and balanced limbs

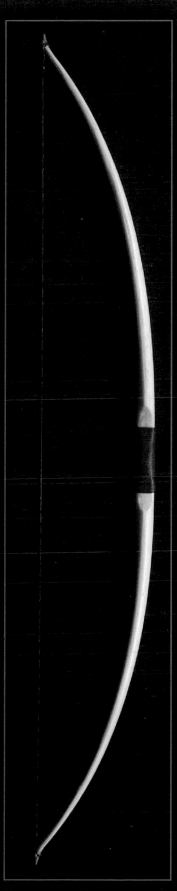

Braced pyramid bow, ash wood/rattan, 55 lbs at 28 inches, length 165 cm

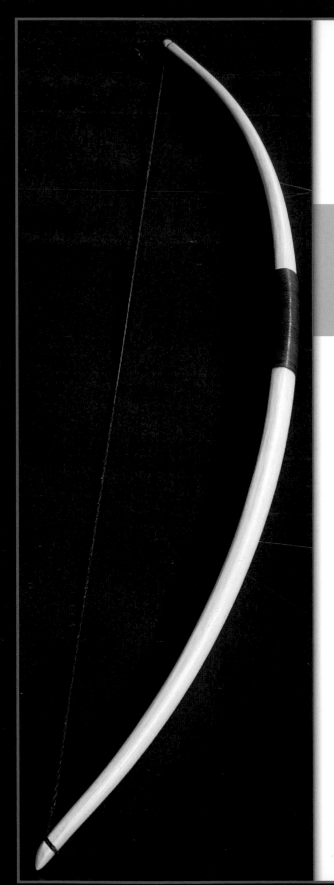

SHORT BOW
of PEARWOOD *and* RATTAN

Type: Short bow
Material: Pearwood and Rattan
Length: ca. 120 cm
Draw weight:
65 lbs at 26 inches draw length

For this short bow we used pearwood for the belly of the bow and rattan for the back of the bow. The nocks are self nocks. The handle area is wrapped with brown buffalo leather lace. With a length of approximately 120 cm, the target was to achieve a draw weight of over 60 lbs at a draw length of 26 inches.

Rattan for the back of the bow: During bending the back of the bow is exposed to tension forces. Because of its elastic properties rattan is particularly suitable to absorb these tension forces.

Pearwood for the belly of the bow: The belly of the bow is more exposed to compression forces during bending. In order to achieve the targeted high draw weight, we reinforced the bow by gluing pearwood veneer to the belly of the bow.

Short bow rattan/pearwood, 65 lbs at 26 inches, length 120 cm

Cutting the
rattan pole with
a band saw

1. Cutting the Rattan Pole

As a first step, we want to cut the rattan pole lengthwise into two equal halves. To prevent the round pole from twisting during sawing, we attach the rattan pole with duct tape to a square timber. Fixed like that, we can place the pole straight and flat on the surface of the band saw table and cut it without any problems.

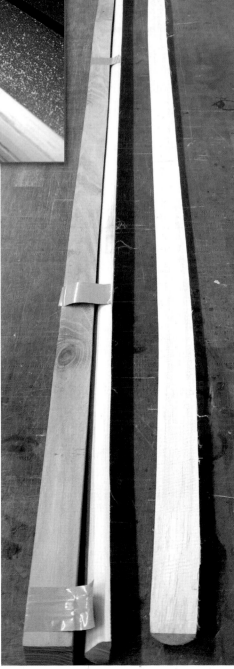

Rattan pole cut
into halves with
"guiding device"

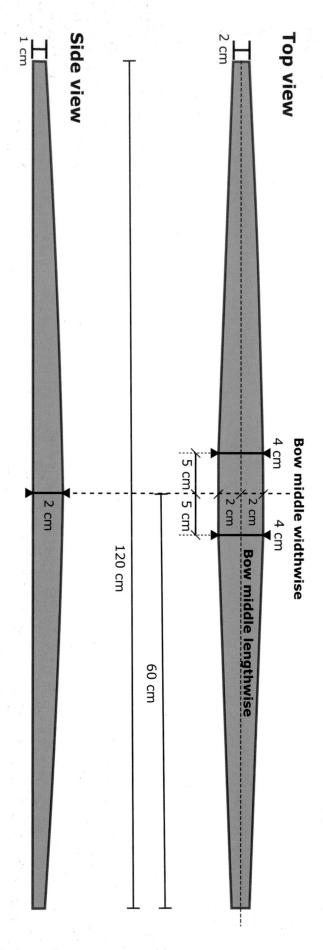

Side view

1 cm

2 cm

120 cm

60 cm

Top view

2 cm

Bow middle widthwise

4 cm

4 cm

2 cm

5 cm

5 cm

2 cm

Bow middle lengthwise

2. Outlining the Bow Profile

We put one of the halves aside for some future project. On the other half of the rattan pole, we will outline the top view and the side view of the bow profile.

For the outlining of the top view we need a string at least 150 cm in length, a 1 m long metal straightedge, and a pencil. First, we cut the rattan pole to the desired length of 120 cm.

Then we mark the bow middle width-wise. Starting from the tips we measure up 60 cm in longitudinal direction and draw a line here. The rattan pole has a diameter of 4 cm. Accordingly, the width in the bow middle is 4 cm as desired.

On this middle marking across the width of the bow, we now make a mark in the middle for the bow middle in longitudinal direction. As a result we get a cross right in the middle of the bow, which we refer to as center mark.

Because a rattan pole is never perfectly straight, we have to determine the bow middle in longitudinal direction with the help of a string that we position lengthwise across the rattan stave, from one end to the other. We make sure that the string runs straight through the center mark and is firmly stretched. The string now indicates the longitudinal bow middle.

At each end of the bow stave we mark the spots where the string rests. Then we draw a straight line from the markings at the tips right through the center mark. This is our center line in longitudinal direction.

Top view outlined on half of the rattan pole

Rattan half after having sawn out the top profile

Now we can easily transfer the dimensions of the top view on the rattan stave. Starting from the lateral middle marking, we measure off 5 cm each to the left and to the right to mark the handle area. In this section we will leave the width at 4 cm.

From the handle area up to the tips we want to taper the width of the bow stave down to 2 cm, so at the tips we mark 1 cm to either side of the center line and draw a connecting line from the markings at the tips to the end of the handle area.

After we have done so for both sides of each limb, we saw out the top profile along the pencil lines.

It is time now for outlining the side profile. Regarding the side view, we have to keep in mind that the rounded outer part of the rattan stave will form the back of the bow and therefore has to remain intact. Starting from the rattan back of the bow, we measure off 1 cm at each end of the bow and make a mark. The bow stave is 2 cm thick in the middle, as desired. So, we extend the lateral center line from the top profile over the edges to the sides, draw a line connecting the middle with the marks at the tips and saw out the side profile along the pencil lines.

Now our rattan stave is prepared for gluing the pearwood veneer to the belly of the bow. The handle area is the broadest and thickest part of the bow stave. From the handle to the tips the rattan stave tapers off in the top view and in the side view.

The toothed blade of the plane leaves fine grooves on the bonding surfaces.

3. Gluing on the Belly of the Bow

For the belly of the bow we have chosen a piece of pearwood veneer, about 6 mm thick, 5 cm wide and of the same length as the rattan stave. The width is bigger than the width of the rattan stave, allowing some margin at the sides for gluing.

Before gluing we roughen the bonding surfaces with a tooth plane and clean and degrease the surfaces with acetone, so that they are clean, dust-free and fat-free.

Caution: Wood dust can be toxic and cause irritation or contact reactions. Acetone can cause damage to your health and is highly flammable. Strictly follow the safety instructions on the container! Take precautionary measures! Always wear appropriate respirator, protective gloves and face protection! Do not use in closed rooms!

The sawed-out rattan stave and a somewhat wider piece of pearwood veneer

A sufficient amount of clamps ensuring a consistent clamping pressure

When the acetone has flashed off well, we apply a two-component glue suitable for highly stressed connections to both bonding surfaces, evenly and according to manufacturer's instructions. Then we place the rattan stave in the middle of the pearwood veneer.

Before we attach the clamps, we cover the stave with a layer of rubber and a piece of veneer, which makes it easier to evenly distribute the pressure and helps to avoid compression marks on our stave.

Starting from the middle, we attach the clamps at regular intervals and tighten them firmly, so that a small amount of glue squeezes out from the joints.

Following the manufacturer's recommendations on compression time, we allow the glue to cure under pressure. Then we remove the clamps and have a look at the result.

A layer of rubber and a piece of veneer lead to a more favorable distribution of clamping pressure and protect the rattan surface against compression marks from the clamps.

Rattan stave and pearwood veneer are glued together firmly. A small amount of glue squeezed out from the joints along the sides. After the appropriate curing time the profile can be adjusted.

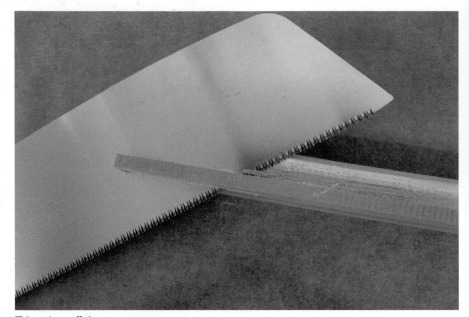

Trimming off the excess veneer

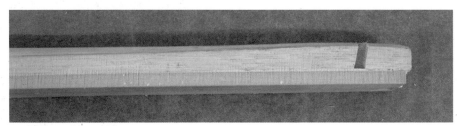

Pearwood veneer (at the bottom) adjusted flush against the rattan backing (at the top)

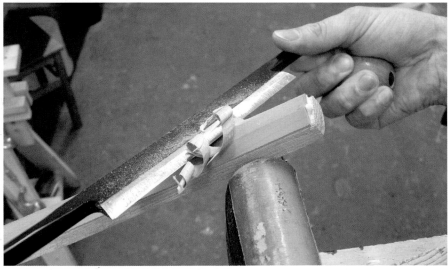

Planing the edges into facets on the pearwood belly

Before we can continue with our work, we have to wait until the curing time according to the manufacturer's instructions has expired and the glue has hardened completely.

After complete curing of the glue, we place the bow stave sideways in the vise and cut the pearwood veneer flush with the rattan backing.

4. Developing an Even Bending

As a preparation for the following tillering steps we use our draw knife to cut inclined facets along the sides of the pearwood veneer on the belly. By planing the edges we obtain a trapeze-like form which will be the basis for the oval shape of the belly of the bow. The middle facet has the biggest impact on the bending, because there the bow stave has its largest diameter. This means that, during tillering, we concentrate on the middle facet when we remove wood from the stiffer sections.

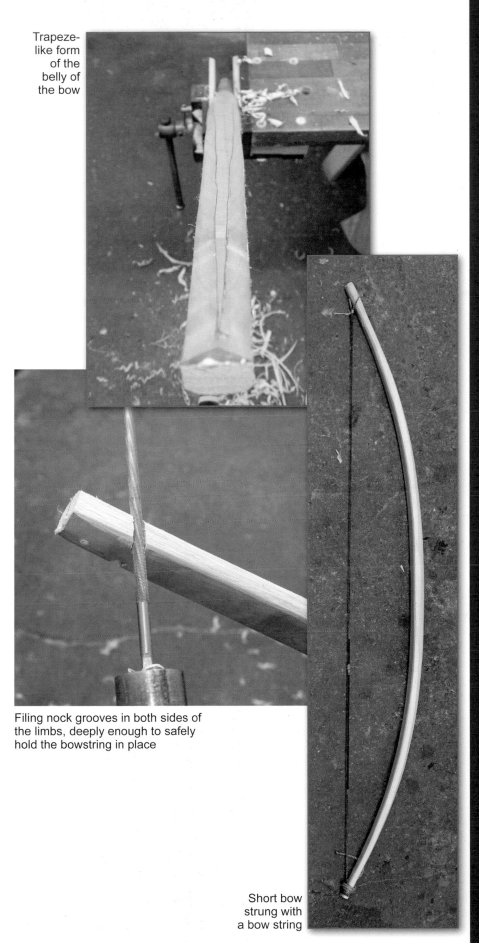

Trapeze-like form of the belly of the bow

Filing nock grooves in both sides of the limbs, deeply enough to safely hold the bowstring in place

Short bow strung with a bow string

We place the bow stave with the bow stringer on the tillering stick, check the bending and mark the stiffer spots where we have to remove some wood. We repeat this procedure until we have achieved an even bending in both limbs.

The tillering process is also described in more detail from page 74 on.

After several tillering steps we want to change from the bow stringer to a bow string. About 2 cm from each end of the bow we cut in nock grooves for holding the bowstring, with a round file (diameter 4 mm).

Now we can brace the bow with the bow string and continue with the tillering, until we have achieved the desired bending and reached the targeted draw weight.

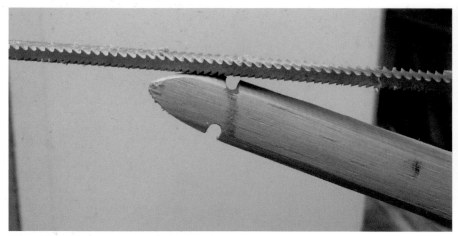

The sides of the nocks tapered into a tip

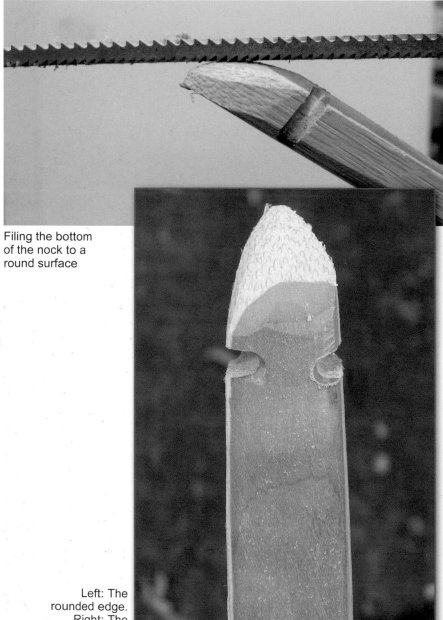

Filing the bottom of the nock to a round surface

Left: The rounded edge. Right: The rough edge

5. Finishing

Our bow is almost finished now - except for the final finishing touches.

To obtain a symmetrical pointed shape at the end of the bow, we round down the nocks on both sides of the limbs towards the middle of the bow. Then we shape the bottom of the nocks into a smooth curve from the belly to the tips and gently plane the edges round.

With a file, we remove any coarse tool marks and carefully round off any remaining edges.

Finally, we sand the surface of our bow beginning with 180-grit sanding paper, then grits 300 and 500, until we have obtained a nice and smooth surface.

For sanding, it is important that we make long movements in longitudinal direction along the belly of the bow. Choppy movements or movements against the longitudinal direction create ugly scratches in the surface that are hard to remove.

After that we thoroughly remove the sanding dust with a paintbrush and evenly coat the entire bow with pure linseed oil. We allow the oil to soak in for a few minutes and then wipe off the excess oil with a cloth. When cured, the linseed oil provides a good surface protection.

Caution: Cloth or brushes soaked with linseed oil are prone to spontaneous combustion and can ignite spontaneously. Never leave them unattended, let them dry outspread on a non-inflammable surface by exposure to air, soak it in water or keep in an airtight container!

In the end, we wrap 3 mm-wide buffalo leather lace around the handle area, and our bow is finished.

Removing the coarse tool marks with a file

Sanding in long movements in a longitudinal direction

Sealing the surface of the bow with linseed oil

Making A Rattan Bow

Handle wrapped with brown buffalo leather lace

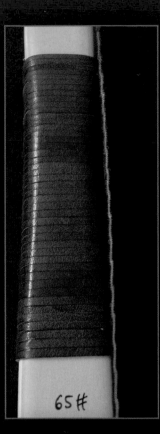

65#

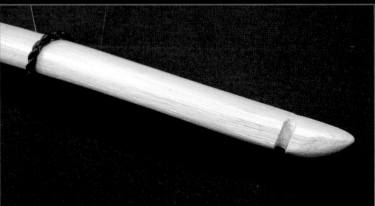

Pointed tips with rounded edges

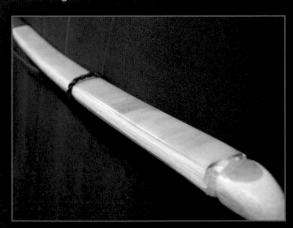

Pearwood belly of the bow

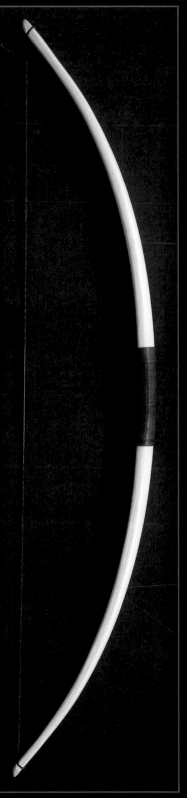

Short bow (65 lbs at 26 inches, length 120 cm) bending through the handle

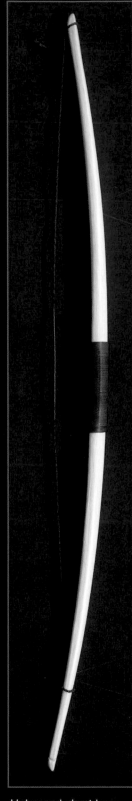

Unbraced short bow

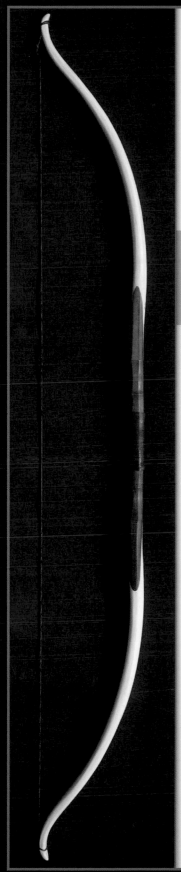

RATTAN RECURVE BOW *with a* WALNUT HANDLE

Type: Recurve Bow
Material: Rattan and Walnut
Length: approx. 170 cm
Draw weight: 45 lbs at 28 inches draw length

Because of its properties (see introduction on page 7), rattan is particularly well suited for building short bows. To take advantage of the full potential of the rattan, it is essential that the bow has a large bending radius. This can easily be achieved for a bow with such short lengths as 120 to 130 cm.

However, these short lengths have an impact on the draw length. When the draw length of a short bow is too large (28 inches or more), the angle between the bow string and the arrow becomes so small that, at full draw, the archer's fingers get pinched.

Another disadvantage of short bow lengths is the unfavorable angle between bow string and tips, which generally leads to an increase in stacking (the disproportionate increase in bow weight perceived during the last few inches before full draw). A good bow should allow a smooth and uniform draw up to full length.

To avoid such negative effects, a bow with a larger draw length should be considerably longer. But, since we do not want to go without the positive properties of the rattan, we simply extend the length of our bow by adding a handle part. The handle part will be stiff, whereas the short limbs of rattan can unfold their full potential.

Rattan recurve bow, 45 lbs at 28 inches,
length 170 cm

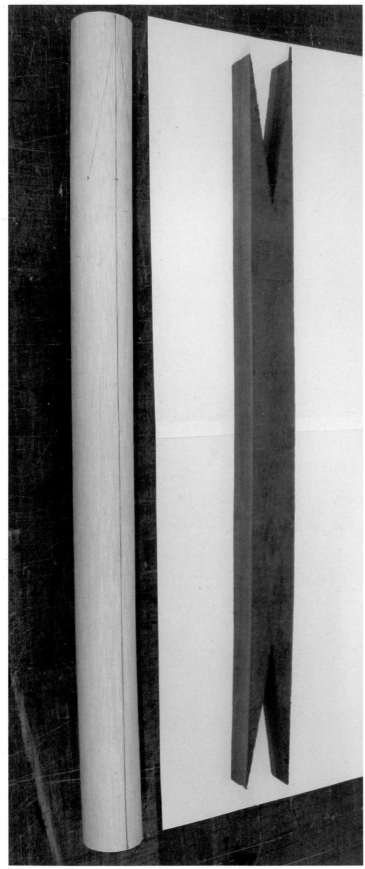

Handle section of walnut and rattan for the bow limbs

1. Splicing Limbs to the Handle

For the stiff handle, we have chosen a piece of walnut wood approximately 50 cm long, 3 cm thick and 4 cm wide, and free of knots and other blemishes or defects that could lead to a breakage of the bow. The two bending limbs of rattan are approximately 60 cm long.

These three parts will now be joined together with a so-called V-splice into a bow stave.

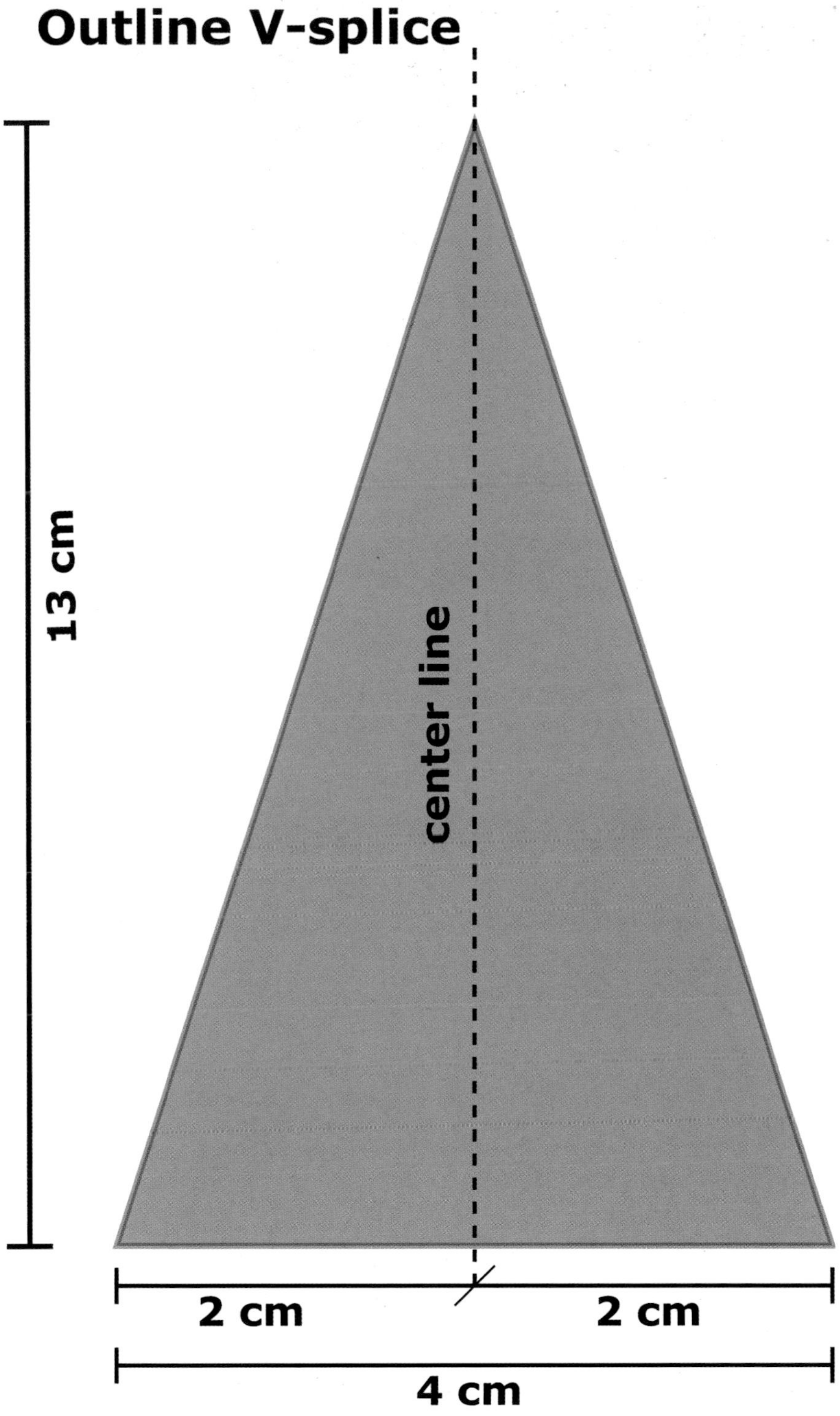

Outline V-splice

13 cm

center line

2 cm

2 cm

4 cm

Dimensions of the V-splice

To a great extent, the stability of adhesive bonds depends on the size of the bonding surfaces. By joining the pieces together with a V-splice, we will obtain larger bonding surfaces and achieve a tight interlocking of the pieces.

For the V-splice, one of the pieces to be glued together has to have a V-shaped cutout at the end, whereas the mating piece has its end cut into a V-shaped wedge. It is essential to achieve a snug fit of both pieces, so that later the glued joint will be straight and even. The more precise the spliced joint is, the lesser the risk that the bow will break during bending.

We start with drawing the center line on the walnut piece for the handle. This will be the basis for outlining the V-splice. From the center line we measure off 13 cm, make a mark there and connect it with the ends of the handle to form a triangle. Then we cut this triangle as straight as possible out of the handle piece.

Making A Rattan Bow

Rattan with outlined V-shape and handle piece of walnut with V-shaped cutout

The V-shaped counterpart cut into the rattan end and the V-shaped cutout in the walnut handle

The V-shaped parts together

As counterparts we use the two 60 cm long round rattan poles (diameter 4 cm) that will form the limbs of the bow. We draw a center line as reference line for the V-splice and transfer the corresponding measurements to the rattan parts. Then we cut, exactly along the lines, the V-shaped wedges into the ends.

Before we start to prepare the surfaces for gluing, we mark all the parts to be glued together with numbers, to make sure that we do not mix them up later. The V-shaped cutout marked with a 1 matches with limb number 1. Accordingly, limb number 2 will fit into the cutout marked with a 2.

After having placed clearly visible marks on all the parts, we can start to adjust the bonding surfaces. For this we need a strip of carbon paper cut into the same width as the bonding surfaces. We fold the strip of carbon paper in the middle and reinforce the fold with a piece of duct tape to make sure that the carbon paper does not get damaged or torn by the sharp edge of the wedge.

A strip of carbon paper folded around the sharp edge of the rattan limb

The V-splice is put together, with carbon paper between the surfaces

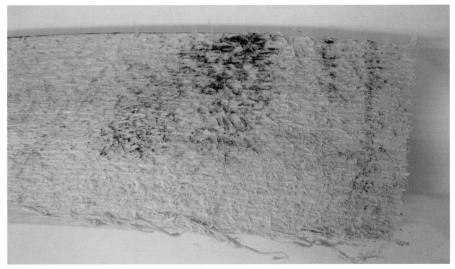

Black marks left by the carbon paper on the rattan limb

We fold a strip of carbon paper around the V-shaped wedge of the limb, with its pigmented side facing inward towards the rattan surface. Then we plug the two mating pieces into each other, as accurately as possible, and press the surfaces together.

To ensure an even adhesion of the glue, it is imperative that the entire bonding surfaces are in close contact with each other. When we now take the pieces apart again, we can see that the carbon paper has left black spots on the contact surfaces, but only in those areas where the surface is not plane, but a little bit convex. In order to obtain a flat surface, we flatten these blackened convex spots carefully with a file.

V-splice pressed together with clamps

V-splice after glue has cured

Now we carry out the same procedure for the surface of the walnut handle. We fold the strip of carbon paper around the edge of the wedge, this time with the pigmented side facing outward towards the walnut surface. Then we plug the two pieces into each other again, and the carbon paper marks the convex spots on the surface which we carefully flatten out with a file.

We repeat this procedure alternately for each surface of the V-splice, until both surfaces have good contact over their total length and fit snugly together.

Before we glue the matching pieces together, we thoroughly clean the bonding surfaces so that they are free of dirt and grease (compare pages 42 to 44).

Caution: Carefully read and follow safety instructions for the use of acetone!

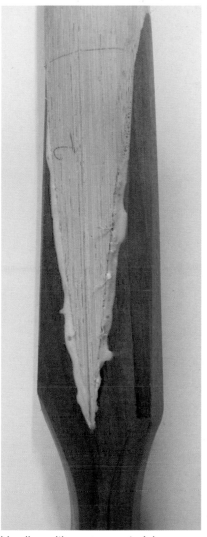

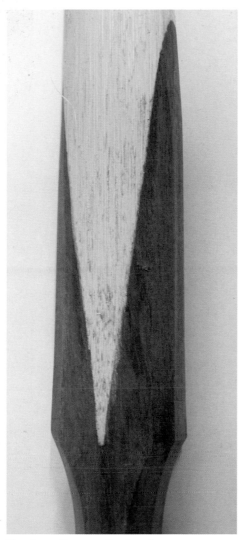

V-splice with excess material
and glue

V-splice with smoothed surface

After cleaning, we apply an appropriate glue uniformly to both bonding surfaces and clamp the pieces together under sufficient pressure. **Follow manufacturer's instructions!**

We apply just enough clamping pressure to squeeze out a small amount of glue from the joints, indicating that we have applied enough glue to ensure good contact between both mating surfaces.

In the same way we proceed with the other limb, and then wait until the glue has completely cured.

After the glue has completely cured, we can start to remove any excess material or glue with a fine rasp. We gently level off the excess on the belly and on the back of the bow, until the surfaces on both sides are neat and smooth. In particular, we take great care to obtain a smooth and even transition from the handle area toward the limbs.

String indicating the "new" center

Marking the width of the limb

Sawing out the width of the rattan limb along the markings

2. Shaping the Limbs

After being glued together, the limbs and handle area should form a straight line along the longitudinal axis of the bow stave. In spite of the special care we had taken during the gluing procedure, our limbs have slightly twisted to one side. This means that we have to draw a new center line before starting to shape the limbs.

We stretch a string over the total length of the bow stave, making sure that it runs straight through the middle of the handle area, exactly over the sharp points of the V-splice. At the end of the bow stave the string does not run through the middle, because the limbs are slightly twisted. So we mark where the string comes to rest at each end, and use these new center marks as reference for laying out the profile of the limbs.

The limb shall start with a width of 4 cm at the end of the handle area and taper down to 2 cm at the tips. Accordingly, we measure 1 cm each to the right and to the left of the new center mark at the tips, mark the width of the limb and draw connecting lines to the ends of the handle area. Then we carefully cut out the top profile of the limb with a saw.

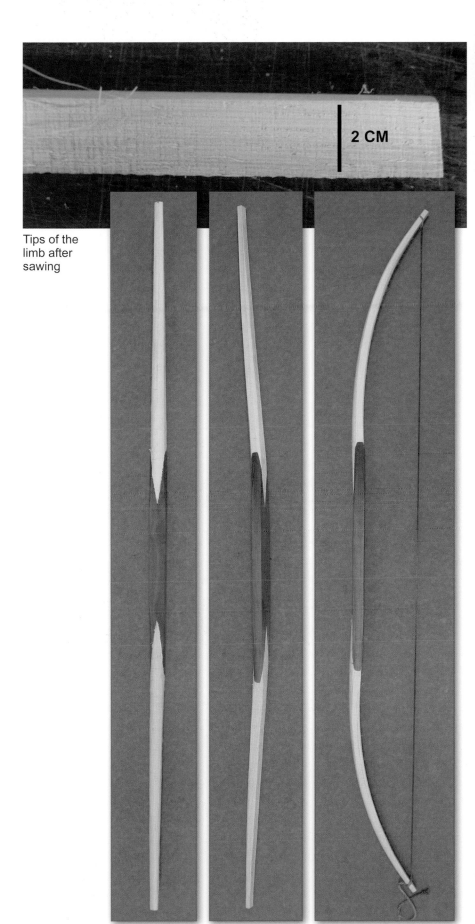

2 CM

Tips of the
limb after
sawing

Top view of
bow stave

Side view of
bow stave

Braced bow stave

After shaping the other limb in the same way, both limbs now taper from 4 cm at the ends of the handle area to 2 cm at the tips (top view).

The next step is to shape the side profile of the limbs. The sides of the limbs should taper to 2 cm at the tips (side view).

Starting from the back of the bow, we mark 2 cm at the tips for the thickness of the limbs. We draw connecting lines between the markings for the thickness and the ends of the handle, and cut out the side profile. The side profile of the limbs now tapers from 3 cm at the handle to 2 cm at the tips.

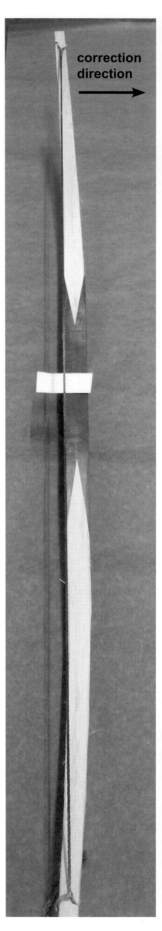

The bow string is off-center to the left

correction direction →

Next, we file the nock grooves for holding the bow string into the tips (see from page 17 on) and brace our bow stave for the first time.

To ensure that the bow fits in the hand comfortably, the bow string should run through the middle of the handle. First of all, we check the position of the bow string on the braced bow. We place the bow on a flat surface with the back facing downwards, so the bow string is facing upwards.

Although we have redetermined the center line and worked thoroughly, the bow string is off-center to the left, because one of the limbs is twisting a little.

To correct this, we will heat the twisted part of the limb and bend it into the right direction, until the bow string runs through the middle of the handle.

On the belly of the twisted limb we mark, with a clearly visible arrow, the direction in which we have to bend the limb.

Then we unbrace the bow again and clamp the handle in the vise.

Corrections near the handle area, even if small, will have an impact on the entire limb. The farther the point, where the bending starts, is away from the handle, the more we would have to bend the limb in order to bring the string back into position. The result would be a visible bending, respectively a hinge in the limb. Accordingly, we carry out the corrections next to the handle area.

However, we have to make sure that the bonding of the V-splice is in no way impaired and does not lose stability due to exposure to high temperatures.

Heating the bending
point on the limb

So, instead of heating with water vapor we will use a hot-air gun, which allows a punctual heating, and we choose a correction point close to the handle, but not directly at the V-splice.

We heat the bending point evenly from all sides with a hot-air gun. Then, we gently bend the limb into the marked direction and leave it in that position to cool off for about five minutes, before we take it out of the vise.

After another 30 minutes, the bow stave has cooled off enough and we can brace it with the bow string again.

Again, we put the back of the bow on a flat surface and look along the sides of the limbs to check the position of the bow string.

Our corrections were successful: The bow string now runs straight through the middle of the handle and the limb does not show any hinges.

In case our first attempt was not successful and the bow string still runs off-center to one side, we have to repeat the procedure.

Bow stave after
correction, with the
string running through
the middle of the handle.

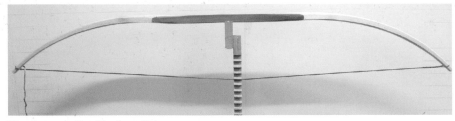

The bow on the tillering stick

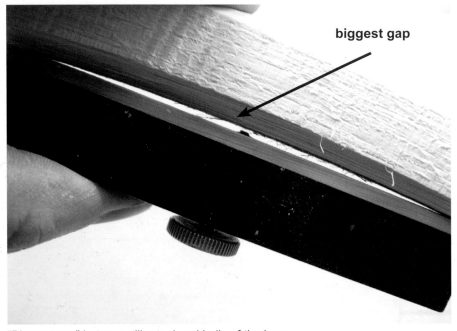

biggest gap

"Biggest gap" between tiller tool and belly of the bow

The pencil integrated in the tiller tool nearly touches the belly of the bow.

3. Tillering

After having adjusted the longitudinal axis of our bow stave, we can start with the tillering process to achieve an even bending of the limbs.

We place the bow stave on the tillering stick. Then we carefully pull the bow string down a little bit, put it in one of the notches and attach a piece of tape next to the notch to mark it as a reference point.

Now we step back a few steps to check the bending of the limbs. Both limbs are already bending more or less evenly, but the bending is not sufficient enough yet. To get the best performance out of the rattan limbs, we want the bending to be considerably stronger and more circular.

For a more accurate check we take the tiller tool and move it along the belly of the bow. In doing so we are looking for the gaps between the tiller tool and the belly. The bigger the gap, the larger is the bending of the limbs in this area. When tillering we never remove any material in the areas where the limbs are bending the most. It is the stiffer areas that we have to weaken by taking off material from the belly, in order to adjust the bending.

We position the tiller tool under the biggest gap, where the limb bends most, and screw out the integrated pencil just so far that it nearly, but not quite touches the belly of the bow. When we move the tiller tool along the belly again, the pencil will mark all the spots where the limbs are bending less than at the "biggest gap."

We slide the tiller tool back and forth along the belly, in long movements from the handle towards

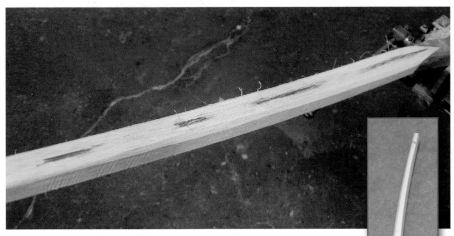

Pencil marks left by the tiller tool on the belly of the bow

The bow stave on the tillering stick, at about 2/3 of the total draw length

The
unbraced
bow after
tillering

the tips. The pencil adjusted to the "biggest gap" now touches all the sections in which the bending radius is smaller, and leaves pencil marks on these stiffer spots.

In the same way we proceed with the other limb. We look for the biggest gap, adjust the pencil lead and mark the stiffer sections where the bending is less.

Then we take the bow stave off the tillering stick and put it in the vise, without bowstring and with the belly of the bow facing upwards. All the sections marked by the pencil are a little bit stiffer than the rest of the limb. To adjust the bending, we use a milled file to remove some material from the marked sections, until all the pencil marks are gone. We work very carefully and make sure to achieve smooth transitions. If we take off too much material, new hinges and uneven transitions will appear on the limbs.

We will repeat this procedure several times now. We place the bow stave back on the tillering stick, pull the bow string down and place it into the next notch, not forgetting to also move the tape accordingly.

At each tillering step we pull the bow string further down and put it in the next notch, because we have to bend the bow a bit more to allow the removal to come into effect.

Then we go on and look for the biggest gap, adjust the tiller tool, mark the stiffer sections and remove material. Now and then we check the draw length and then continue with the tillering, until both limbs are bending evenly and we have reached the targeted draw length.

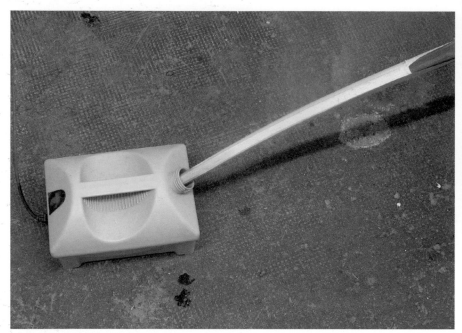

End of the bow in boiling water

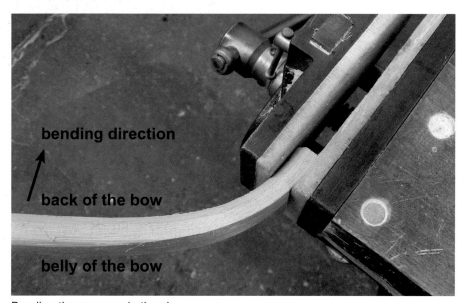

bending direction

back of the bow

belly of the bow

Bending the recurves in the vise

4. Bending the Recurves and Re-tillering

Now that the tillering of the bow is practically finished, we are going to bend the recurves into the limbs. After we have done so, the tiller will have changed again and we have to do some re-tillering.

Before bending the recurves, we have to heat the rattan to make it more flexible. Since there are no glue bondings at the ends of the limbs, we use a water boiler to heat the rattan.

We leave the ends of the bow in boiling water for about three minutes. Then we clamp the last 3 cm of the tips in the vise and carefully bend the bow in shooting direction, away from the archer, until we have reached the desired bending radius for the recurves. Now we keep the bow in this position for a few minutes.

After that we have to check the longitudinal axis of the bow again. At the tip the bow is slightly twisted. Because the rattan has not yet totally cooled off, we can gently bend the tip back towards the longitudinal axis without affecting the bending of the recurves.

The bow with
outward bent
limbs, facing
away from the
archer (recurves)

The bow with recurves during retillering

After bending two equally shaped recurves into the ends of the limbs, we leave the bow to dry for about two to three days. The rattan has to dry off sufficiently, because otherwise the recurves will come off when put under stress during re-tillering.

For re-tillering, we brace the bow with the bow string again and place it on the tillering stick. Then we check the bending. The shaping of the recurves has caused only small changes in the tiller.

Again, we use the tiller tool to mark the stiffer spots and find that only small corrections are necessary. The more advanced the tillering stage, the greater is the impact of removing material. Therefore, we are especially careful during re-tillering and take off only very small amounts. We continue with the tillering, until we are happy with the bending of the limbs.

The bow after re-tillering

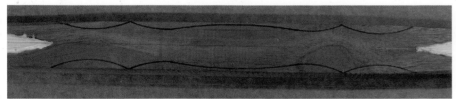

Outlined contours for the handle

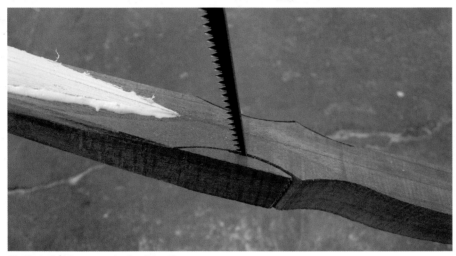

Cutting tight curves in the handle

Cut-out shape of the handle

Now our bow is ready to be test-shot for the first time. After test-shooting we check the tiller once again to make sure that the bending stress has not caused any more changes in the tiller. If this should be the case, we have to do some more re-tillering. But with our bow everything is alright: The limbs are bending nice and smooth.

5. Shaping the Handle and Finishing

In order to make it easier to clamp the bow stave in the vise during tillering, we had provisionally kept the square shape of the handle. But now we will bring the handle to its final shape, and there are almost no limits to our imagination. The only thing we have to keep in mind is that we do not make the handle area too narrow, because otherwise the handle will be bending when the bow is drawn.

We outline the shape of the handle and use a small saw to carefully cut the tight curves of the shape.

Beveling the edges of the handle with a rasp

Rounding-off the recurves with a rasp

Using a rasp or a file, we bevel the edges of the handle into slightly inclined facets which we then round off into a smooth curve.

The handle still has a rough surface with small sawing marks on it. We smooth out the surface with a file, until it looks nice and harmonious.

Then we also round off the slightly angular recurves, until we obtain an even and uniform transition into the limbs. We taper the ends of the bow into smoothly pointed tips, making sure that the nock grooves are sufficiently deep and do not have sharp edges.

And finally the finishing touches: We sand the entire bow with sanding paper of grit 180, 300 and 500, and then oil the surface with tung oil as protective coating.

In the end, our bow gets a handle wrapping with brown buffalo leather lace.

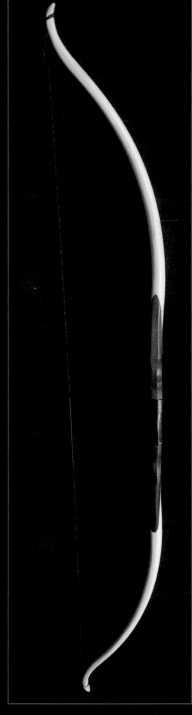

Unbraced rattan recurve bow

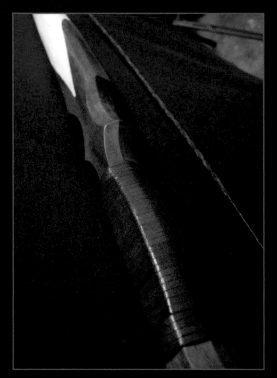

Handle with rounded facets and buffalo leather wrapping

Rattan recurve bow with walnut handle, 45 lbs at 28 inches

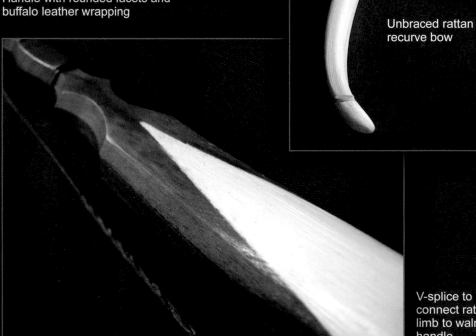

V-splice to connect rattan limb to walnut handle

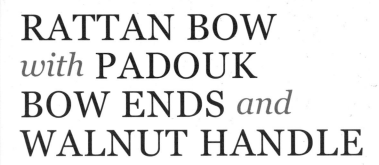

RATTAN BOW *with* PADOUK BOW ENDS *and* WALNUT HANDLE

Type: Longbow
Material: Rattan, Padouk and Walnut
Length: approx. 160 cm
Draw weight: 35 lbs at 29 inches

In principle, this bow design is very much the same as the design of the rattan recurve with walnut handle from page 63.

The handle is stiff and does not bend when the bow is drawn. The working rattan limbs are extended with stiff limbs made of padouk.

This is what we need for the V-splices:
- one piece of walnut for the handle (approx. 50 cm long, 4 cm wide and 3 cm thick)
- two round rattan poles (each approx. 50 cm long, 4 cm wide and 4 cm thick)
- two pieces of padouk for the ends (each approx. 20 cm long, 2.5 cm wide and 2 cm thick)

By connecting the pieces together, we can achieve a total bow length of 160 cm, which has a positive effect on the obtainable draw length and the angle between bow string and tips. At the same time it is possible to reach a high bending radius of the working rattan limbs, thus making the most of the positive bending properties of the rattan.

Longbow with padouk ends, rattan limbs, and walnut handle; 35 lbs at 29 inches; length 160 cm

Outline V-splice

13 cm

center line

2 cm   2 cm

4 cm

1. Making the V-Splices

Now we are going to attach the single pieces together into a bow stave. The width of the components is a little bit larger than necessary, to allow for potential adjustments later on. We draw the top view of the V-splices on the wide sides of the components, whereas the thick sides are used as the basis for the side profile.

First of all, we want to attach the walnut handle to the rattan limbs. We draw center lines, as reference lines for the V-splice, onto the wide sides of the corresponding pieces. As described in further detail from page 64 on, we transfer the dimensions of the V-splice and cut each component to the required shape. Before we apply the glue and press the corresponding pieces together with clamps, we thoroughly smooth the mating surfaces.

Outlining the V-splice

The finished V-splice

After the glue has completely cured, we prepare the padouk ends of the bow for gluing. Just to avoid any confusion we erase the current center lines from the handle and from the limbs, because for the next V-splices we have to determine new center lines.

Again, we place a string along the entire length of the bow stave. To ensure a nice and symmetrical shape of the V-splices, the center line has to run straight through the middle of the handle, exactly across the sharp points of the V-splices. Accordingly, we align the string with the center of the V-splice.

At the ends of the limbs the string is off-center, because the bow stave is slightly twisted after gluing. Since from the outset we left some room for adjusting the width, we will deal with that later.

The center line serves as a reference line just for the V-splice. Thus, we do not need to draw the whole center line on the limbs, but only the first 20 cm. So we mark the position of the string at the end and at 20 cm from the end, and draw a straight line between the markings.

In doing so, it is essential to make sure that the string does not get out of place, but runs exactly over the middle of the handle.

Having drawn the new center lines in this way on both limbs, we now outline the dimensions of the V-splice between the rattan limbs and the padouk ends of the bow.

Erasing the "old" center line

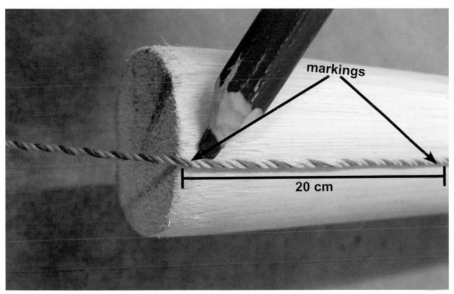

Marking of the new center line

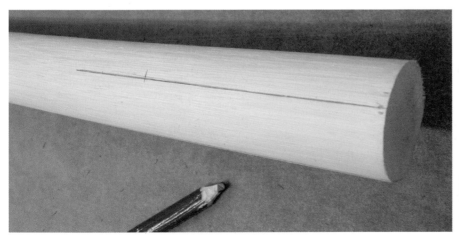

The new center line for the V-splice

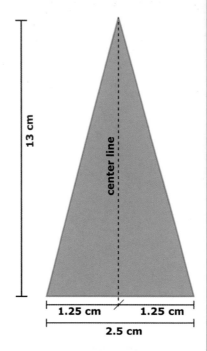

13 cm

center line

1.25 cm | 1.25 cm

2.5 cm

The same principle as before: The V-splice shall be 13 cm long, as the previous one, whereas the width of the V-splice needs to be compliant with the width of the padouk components we have chosen, which is 2.5 cm. Accordingly, we mark 13 cm lengthwise and 1.25 cm to each side of the center line and connect the markings into a triangle.

Outlining the V-splice

Marking the V-splice

The V-splice outlined on the rattan limb, on the back of the bow

The next step is to transfer the same dimensions, but mirrored on the padouk counterpart.

Prior to sawing the contours of the V-splice we have to adjust the side profile. The rattan limbs are still round and have a thickness of 4 cm, whereas the padouk ends of the bow are 2 cm thick.

The sides of the limbs shall taper from 3 cm in the handle area to 2 cm at the tips (side view). Correspondingly, we reduce the thickness at the belly of the bow. The back of the bow, with the dimensions on it, keeps its round shape.

For the thickness of the limbs, we measure off 2 cm at the end of each limb and mark the points on the belly of the bow from where the walnut handle starts. Then we connect the markings with straight lines and cut out the side profile of the limbs evenly along the lines. When we cut off the excess rattan at the V-spliced handle, we take care not to cause any damage to the V-splice.

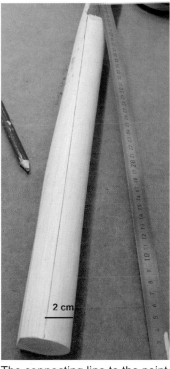

Outlining the side profile

The connecting line to the point where the handle starts

The sawed-out side profile

Cut out V-shapes for the splice between the rattan limb and the padouk end of the bow.

Adjusting the surface with carbon paper

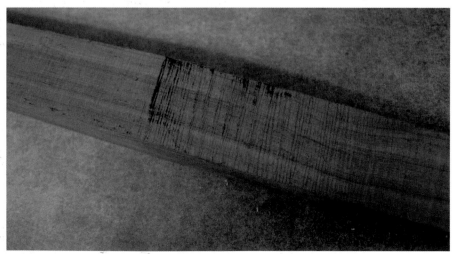

Uneven spots marked by the carbon paper

Having adjusted the side profile of both limbs, we can now cut out the contours for the V-splice between the rattan limbs and the padouk end of the bow.

Prior to gluing we have to adjust the bonding surfaces, as described in more detail from page 66 on. To prevent accidental mixing of the single parts during and after adjustment, we mark the right limb and the corresponding padouk part with a 1, the rattan and the padouk parts for the left limb with a 2.

To obtain smooth and even bonding surfaces, we now try to locate the uneven spots which have to be smoothed off. We put a stripe of carbon paper between the bonding surfaces and press the parts together. The carbon paper marks the uneven or convex spots on the surface which we carefully level with a file.

Now we turn the carbon paper over to mark the uneven spots on the other bonding surface and level the blackened spots with a file. We repeat these steps, until we have achieved a snug fit of the mating surfaces.

Leveling the round sides of the limbs

Gluing the padouk ends in place

Finished
bow stave

Since the sides of the rattan limbs are still round in the area of the V-splice, it is impossible to properly attach the clamps that have to hold everything in position and provide the needed clamping pressure. Thus, we use the draw knife to slightly level the sides of the rattan limbs in the area of the V- splice, until the surface is straight enough to attach the clamps.

After all this preparation, we can start with the gluing of the V-splice: First, we carefully read the manufacturer's instructions on the materials we want to use for gluing. **Follow the safety instructions!**

We clean and degrease the surfaces to be bonded (see also from page 42 onward).

Next, we coat the surfaces with an appropriate glue and press the parts together, applying uniform clamping pressure to the V-splice. In order to be confident that the glue is evenly distributed over the entire surface, we make sure that a small amount of glue squeezes from the joints.

We wait for the time advised in the manufacturer's instructions and remove the clamps. Before we can continue to work on our bow stave, we have to wait until the glue has completely cured.

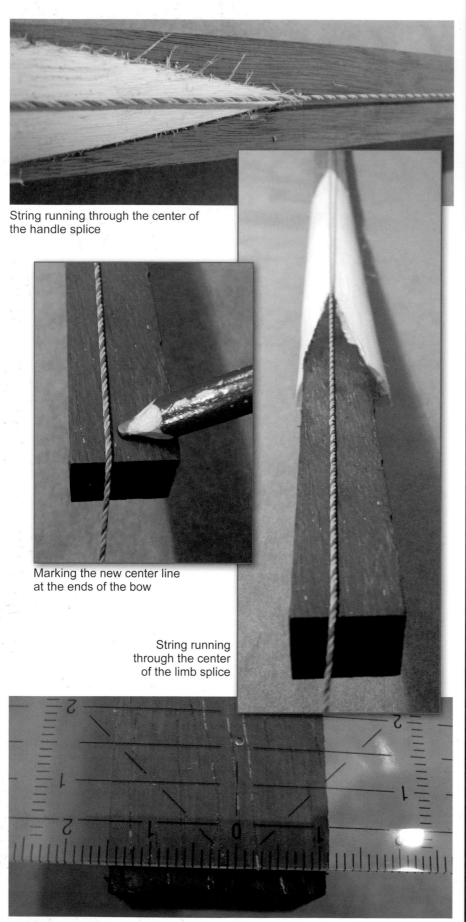

String running through the center of
the handle splice

Marking the new center line
at the ends of the bow

String running
through the center
of the limb splice

The new center line at 0 and markings for the width of the limbs

2. Shaping and Tillering

Finally, our bow stave is ready for shaping and tillering.

Before we can carve the nock grooves that hold the bow string in place, we have to adjust the glued-in padouk ends of the bow. Again, we determine the center line by placing a string over the entire length of the bow stave making sure it runs straight through the middle over the sharp points of the V-splice.

It has paid off that we worked very thoroughly and determined a new center line for each gluing step: the string runs straight through the middle of the V-splices both in the handle area and at the limbs.

At the padouk ends of the bow, the string is off-center. We make a mark to the left and to the right of the string for the new center line.

The markings for the new center line serve as a reference for the outlining of the bow ends. Since we have chosen a width of 1.6 cm for the tips, we mark 8 mm each to the left and to the right of the center (see picture below left).

Contours at the bow ends

Side view of the nock groove

Limb with nock groove

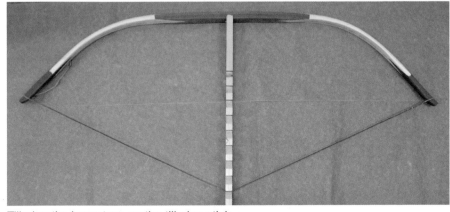

Side view of the bow stave after gluing and shaping

The braced bow stave

Tillering the bow stave on the tillering stick

As seen in the picture at top left, we draw connecting lines between the markings for the width and the beginning of the V-splice. Then we cut out the contours of the padouk ends along the connecting lines.

Using a file, we give a round shape to the padouk ends and remove the excess rattan from the sides, until we have achieved a harmonious transition between the rattan limbs and the padouk ends.

To also obtain smooth surfaces on the belly and the back of the bow, we file off the excess rattan or glue left around the V-splice.

Now we can carve the nock grooves into the tips, which will hold the bow string in place. Using a round file (diameter 4 mm) we file vertical grooves into the back of the bow stave. To ensure a safe fit, we file the nock grooves at a slight angle towards the sides, making sure that the nock grooves are sufficiently deep and rounded at the edges.

Finally we can brace our bow for the first time.

At first glance, our bow stave looks quite nice: the bow does not bend in the walnut handle, neither at the padouk ends of the bow. As a result of the repeated replacing of the center line and the thorough adjusting of the profile, the rattan limbs are bending quite evenly and the balance between the limbs looks fine.

Next, we are going to check the result at the tillering stick. As described in further detail from page 74 on, we look along the rattan limbs to find the biggest gaps between the tiller tool and the belly of the bow, indicating the sections in which the limb bends more than in the adjacent areas.

Thanks to our accurate preparation there are only relatively small gaps. We mark the stiffer spots on the limbs with the tiller tool.

The further advanced we are in the tillering process, in other words the more the bow bends, the bigger are the effects of removing material. Accordingly, we use a fine file to take off only small amounts of rattan from the stiffer spots and immediately check the result at the tillering stick.

We do not remove any material in the handle area or at the padouk ends, because we want these sections of the bow to be stiff and not bending.

Now we repeat the tillering steps (finding and marking the stiffer spots, removing material), until we have reached the targeted draw length. After each tillering step we bend the bow a little bit more and check the effects of the removal of material.

When we have achieved the desired draw length and both limbs are bending evenly, we sand the surface with sanding paper of grit 180, 300 and 500. Then we round down any unpleasant edges in the handle area and at the padouk ends, until our bow has a nice and well-balanced shape.

Again, we use tung oil as surface protection. We apply the tung oil evenly to the surface of the whole bow and let it dry off well.

Caution: Follow safety instructions (see also page 50)!

In the end we add a nice vegetable-tanned laced leather grip around the handle (see more details from page 36 on).

Belly of the bow

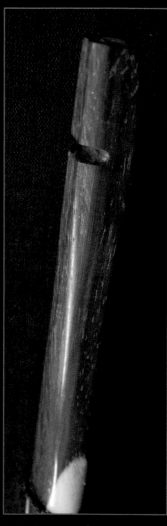

Padouk bow ends

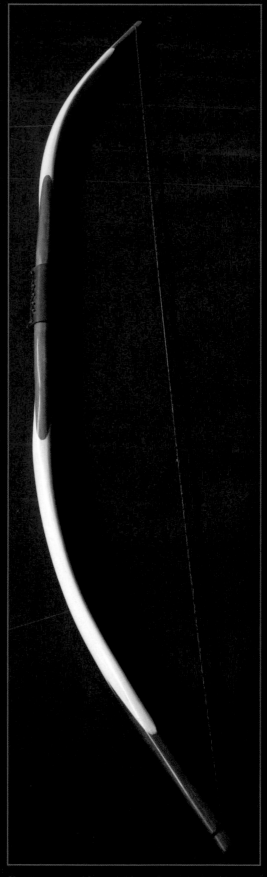

Rattan bow with padouk ends and walnut handle, 35 lbs at 29 inches, length 160 cm

Walnut handle

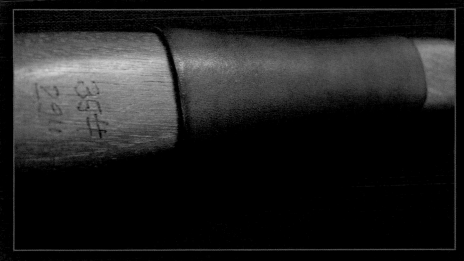

Vegetable-tanned leather grip

RATTAN RECURVE BOW *with* PEARWOOD HANDLE *and* LAMINATED RECURVES

Type: Recurve bow
Material: Rattan, Pearwood, Ash wood and Lacewood
Length: ca. 170 cm
Draw weight: 30 lbs at 29 inches

In this bow design, again, handle area and ends of the bow are stiff and do not bend, whereas the rattan forms the working part of the limbs. The handle is a little bit shorter this time. Instead, we have increased the length of the working rattan limbs in order to fully exploit the bending capacity of the rattan. The ends of the bow are laminated from three layers of veneer and bent into recurves. To optimize the position of the bow string, we add string grooves to the recurves.

For this bow design we need:
- one piece of pearwood for the handle (approx. 30 cm long, 6 cm wide and 3 cm thick)
- two round rattan poles (each approx. 60 cm long, 4 cm wide and 4 cm thick)
- two strips of ash wood veneer (each approx. 50 cm long, 3 cm wide and 0.5 cm thick)
- four strips of lacewood veneer (each approx. 50 cm long, 3 cm wide and 0.5 cm thick)

As with the previously presented bows, the different components of the bow are glued together with V-splices. In the course of the gluing process the laminated bow ends are bent into recurves.

Bow with laminated recurves (ash wood and lacewood), rattan limbs and pearwood handle, 30 lbs at 29 inches, length 170 cm

1. V-Splice for the Handle

A more detailed description on how to make a V-splice is given from page 64 on.

First, we determine and outline the center lines on the rattan parts and on the pearwood piece for the handle. Using the center lines as reference lines for the V-splice between the handle and the limbs, we transfer the dimensions and cut out the shapes of the V-splice.

Before we start gluing, we thoroughly adjust the bonding surfaces by placing carbon paper between the components to be glued together. The carbon paper leaves black traces on the areas from which to remove some material. We turn the carbon paper over to mark the uneven areas on the opposite bonding surface and level them with a file. We continue to do so until we have achieved the best possible fit.

The more accurate we are in making the adjustments, the lower is the risk that the bonding cannot withstand the stress put on it when the bow is drawn.

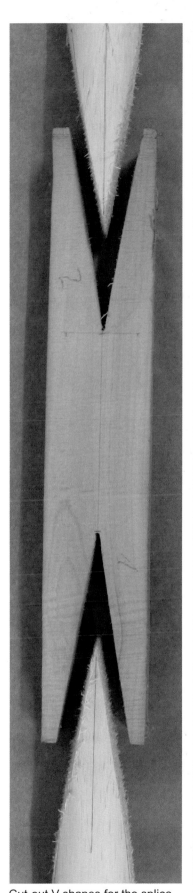

Cut-out V-shapes for the splice between limb and handle

Snug fit of the components

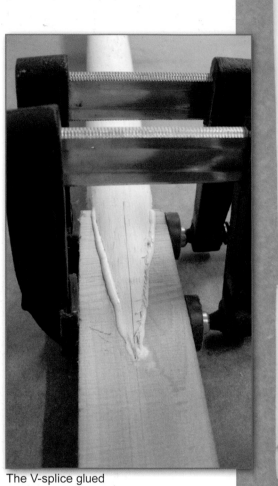

The V-splice glued together

After adjustment of the bonding surfaces, we thoroughly clean off any dirt and dust and degrease the surfaces with acetone.

Caution: Follow all safety precautions when working with solvents!

When the acetone has evaporated off, we can begin with the gluing. We apply a sufficient amount of glue to the bonding surfaces and clamp the components of the V-splice together. In order to obtain a good adhesion, we make sure to use enough clamping pressure to squeeze out some glue from the joints.

Once the compression time has elapsed, we remove the clamps and let the glue cure completely.

Caution: Observe the manufacturer's instructions!

Top view of the V-splice between the limbs and handle

Side view of the V-splice between the limbs and handle

The string is running exactly over the sharp points of the V-splice.

The string is off-center at the ends of the bow stave

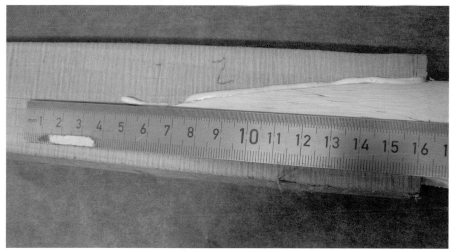

The new center line is running through the middle of the V-splice

2. Laminating and Splicing the Recurves

To ensure that the recurves can be properly positioned along the longitudinal axis, we have to determine and outline the new center line. We place a string over the entire length of the bow stave, making sure that it runs straight through the middle, right over the sharp points of the V-splice.

When we glued the splice between the handle and the rattan limbs, the limbs have twisted slightly to the sides, so that the bow string is off-center at the ends of the bow stave. At the points where the string rests, we mark the starting points of the new center line.

Drawing the center line

Veneer strips
for the recurves

Veneer strips
bent into
recurves
before gluing

Since we just need the center line as a reference line for outlining the V-splice, we do not have to draw the whole center line, but need to mark only the first 20 cm of it.

We place a ruler exactly on the new center mark at the ends. As the rounded surface of the rattan limbs makes it difficult to draw a straight line, we use a spring clamp to hold the ruler in place. Before we draw a straight line along the ruler, we make sure again that it runs exactly through the middle of the V-splice.

In case the ruler got out of position and the center line is not straight, we have to erase the drawn line and try again.

To create a nice visual contrast, we have chosen to use bright ash wood for the middle and dark lacewood for the outsides of the laminated recurves. For bending the recurves we have built a wooden form with the desired bending radius.

First we roughen the bonding surfaces with a tooth plane. Since the veneer is relatively thick (5 mm), we have to heat the wood to make it more flexible. We put the strips of veneer halfway in a pot of boiling water for about five minutes. When we place the veneer strips in the right order on top of each other, we keep in mind that the non-roughened surfaces have to be at the outside. After heating, the veneer strips are flexible enough to be bent over the prepared form and fastened with clamps.

Before removing the clamps, we let the veneer strips cool off in the form for about 15 minutes. Now the recurves have to dry for at least one day, before we can continue.

Once the recurves have dried completely, we thoroughly clean and degrease the bonding surfaces—as already described on pages 56 to 58—

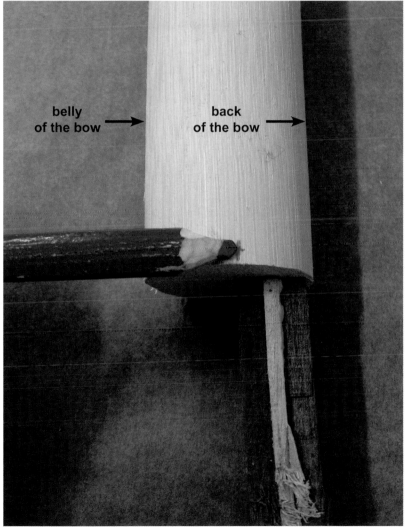

The bent veneer strips glued together, wrapped in plastic wrap, and secured with duct tape

belly
of the bow →   back
of the bow →

Marking the thickness, recurves being flush with the back of the bow

and apply an appropriate glue. We place the veneer strips in the same order as before, on top of each other, and wrap them in plastic wrap, to avoid any glue getting between the recurves and the wooden form when we attach the clamps. To prevent the veneer strips from slipping sideways, we secure them with duct tape.

We put back the recurves, wrapped in this way, over the wooden form and firmly, but carefully, fasten them with clamps. Now we leave the recurves in the form for several hours or, better, overnight. The next day we remove the clamps and the plastic wrap and let the glue cure completely.

When the glue has completely dried, we can continue to work on the recurves. First we cut them to the desired length, so that the ends of the veneer strips are flush with each other. Then we remove all excess glue and excess veneer from the sides, until the recurves have a smooth surface and a rectangular cross section.

Before we can glue the splice between the recurves and the rattan limbs, we have to adjust the side profile of the limbs. The limbs have to taper from the handle area to the thickness of the recurves.

Because the back of the bow is exposed to tension, it is essential not to damage the grain structure of the rattan on the back of the bow. Thus, the back of the bow will keep its rounded shape and we will reduce the thickness of the limbs on the belly side of the bow.

Accordingly, we place the recurves flush to the back of the bow and mark the thickness of the recurves at the end of the rattan limb.

Outlining the
side profile
at the end of
the limb

Outlining the
side profile
at the end of
the handle

Measuring half
the width of
the recurves to
either side of the
center line

V-splice
outlined on the
rattan limb

V-splice
outlined on the
rattan limb and
corresponding
conterpart on
the recurves

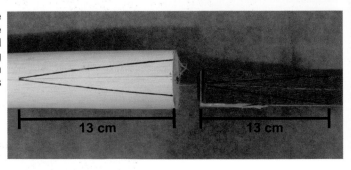

Starting from this marking, we draw a straight connecting line along the edge of the ruler to the end of the handle. Then, we saw out the side profile of the limb along this line.

Likewise, we cut the side profile of the other limb to shape. Both limbs now taper from the thickness of the handle to the thickness of the recurves (side view).

Both rattan limbs are ready for splicing now: We have drawn a center line on their back and have prepared the side profile. The next thing we have to do is to draw the center line on the recurves. We mark the middle at the end of the non-bent section of the recurves and draw the center line.

Again, we use the center lines as reference lines for outlining the dimensions of the V-splice. We measure up 13 cm on the center line for the length of the V-splice. As the width has to match the width of the recurves, we measure off half the width of the recurves to either side of the center line and connect the markings into the triangle shape of the V-splice.

Cut-out V-shapes before adjusting the surfaces

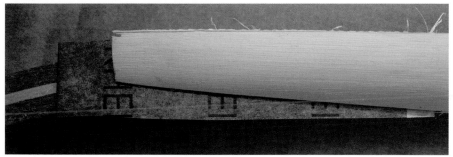

Carbon paper placed between the surfaces

Uneven sections on the rattan surface

Blackened sections on the surface of the recurves

Parts of the V-splice fitting together perfectly

Having outlined the dimensions of the V-splices for both limbs, we cut out the V-shapes exactly along the marked lines.

To achieve a durable adhesion that can withstand the bending stress it will be exposed to later, it is imperative to ensure good contact between the surfaces. Therefore we have to adjust the surfaces to be bonded together. First we mark the mating parts of the left and of the right V-splice with numbers, so we do not mix them up during or after adjustment of the surfaces.

Again, we use carbon paper to mark the uneven sections that need to be levelled out. We place the carbon paper between the mating surfaces of the V-splice and remove a little material from the blackened sections. Then we turn the carbon paper over to mark the uneven sections on the opposite bonding surface. We carefully level them out with a file and repeat the procedure until the corresponding parts fit into each other perfectly.

Gluing of the V-splice

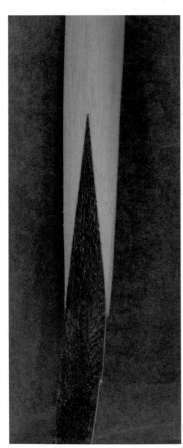

"Floating" transition from the limb into the recurves

Top view of glued-up bow stave

Side view of glued-up bow stave

Prior to gluing, we slightly flatten the round surface of the rattan limbs on the sides of the V-splice so that we get a straight surface to which we can attach the clamps.

The gluing procedure is described in more detail from page 42 onward.

Caution: Read the manufacturer's instructions carefully! Follow the safety instructions and take appropriate safety precautions!

After thorough cleaning and degreasing of the surfaces, we apply a sufficient amount of glue to the bonding surfaces.

After the glue is applied, we attach the clamps around the V-splice and press the components together firmly, making sure that some glue squeezes out all along the joint.

When the glue has fully cured, we remove the excess glue from around the V-splice and carefully level off the excess on the rattan limbs until we achieve a floating transition between the limbs and the recurves.

Now that our bow stave has been glued up successfully, we can pass on to the next step.

3. Shaping the Recurves

As with the previous steps, we first determine the new center line to check if the bow stave has developed any twists during the gluing procedure.

We put the bow stave on a plane surface, with the recurves facing upwards. Since we do not have a plane surface on which the string can be placed, we lay the string over both ends of the recurves, so that it sags over the total length of the bow and hangs loosely about 5 mm above the handle area.

To align the string in the middle of the handle, we gently move it across the ends of the recurves until it runs straight over the sharp points of the V-splice. After a few attempts we have managed to position the string in the right place. We mark the position of the string at the ends of the recurves. This is the center mark for the new bow middle.

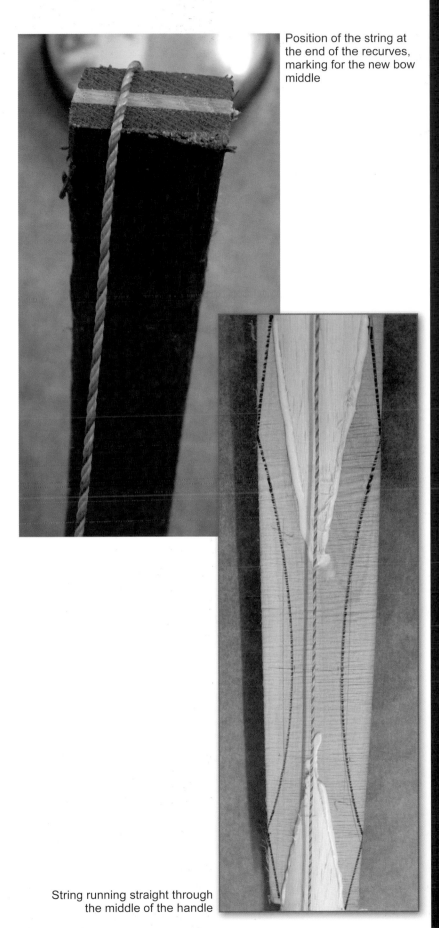

Position of the string at the end of the recurves, marking for the new bow middle

String running straight through the middle of the handle

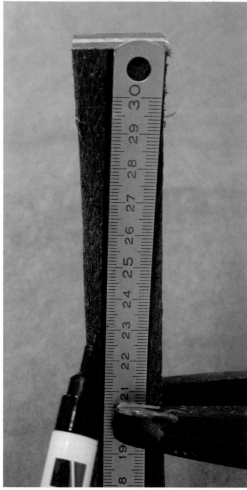

Outlining the new outer edge of the limb

Center mark for new bow middle

A　　　　B

Marking for the new outer edge

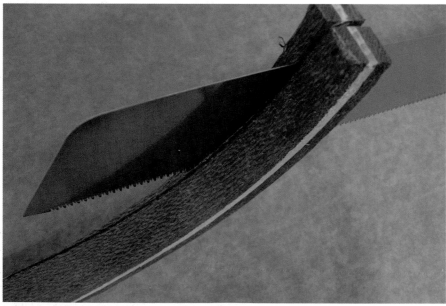

Sawing out the recurves along the marked line

This new center mark will be used as reference point for outlining the shape of the recurves. Since at the outset we made the recurves slightly wider than necessary, we now have enough room for adjustment.

Taking the center mark as the basis for the new bow middle, we now determine the width of the recurves. The outer edge with the larger distance to the bow middle (A) can be adjusted, whereas it is not possible to remove much material from the outer edge with the smaller distance to the bow middle (B). We have to leave the width of the outer edge (B) like it is. This means that the distance from (B) to the bow middle is equal to half the width of the end of the recurves.

Accordingly, we mark the same distance on the other side of the center mark and draw a straight connecting line from the marking to the beginning of the V-splice. Thus, we now have a new outer edge for the shape of the recurves, with both sides being symmetrical and having the same width.

In the same way, we determine the width of the recurves at the other end of the bow, and saw out the shapes along the marked lines.

Then we check the width of both recurves. If the widths at the bow ends largely differ in size, we have to adjust them accordingly. When we carefully remove a small amount of material from the wider side, we keep an eye on the center line to make sure that both sides are symmetrical to each other along the center line.

Filing the nock grooves at the end of the recurves

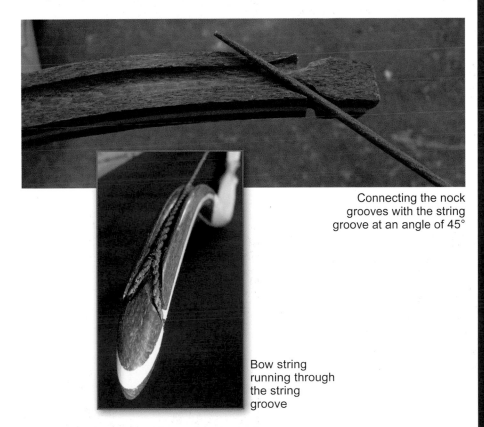

Using a rasp to carve the string groove in the middle of the recurves

Connecting the nock grooves with the string groove at an angle of 45°

Bow string running through the string groove

Next are the nock grooves for holding the bow string in place: Using a round file (diameter 4 mm), we file the nock grooves into both sides of the recurves - at a distance of 2 cm from the end and at an angle of about 30°, making sure that the grooves are sufficiently deep and on the same level.

At the curved ends the bow string tends to slip sideways out of position. To keep the bow string in the middle, we will carve string grooves into the recurves.

The removal of material will also lead to a reduction in the weight of the recurves, and thus an improvement in the efficiency of the bow, because the mass to be moved is smaller.

We use a round rasp (diameter 8 mm) to carve the string grooves on the belly side of the bow. The string groove starts about 0.5 cm away from the nock grooves and runs straight through the middle all along the length of the recurves. We remove all marks left by the rasp and smooth the surface of the string groove with a round file of the same diameter.

To connect the nock grooves on the sides with the string groove on the belly, we carve a groove at an angle of about 45° making sure that the grooves are symmetrical and smoothly merge into each other.

Since any sharp edges on the string groove or the nock grooves could cause severe damage to the bow string when the bow is braced, we carefully round off the sharp edges.

As described in more detail from page 49 on, we shape the ends of the recurves into curved, slightly pointed tips.

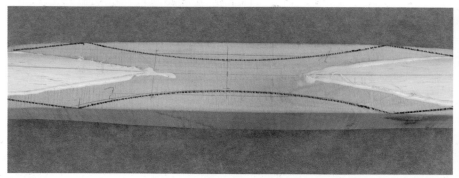

Outlined shape of the handle

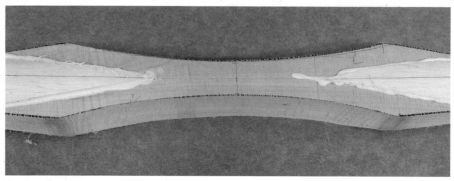

Cut-out handle

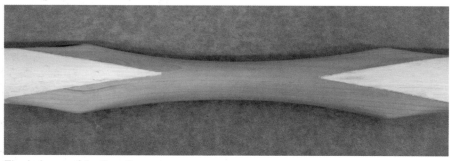

Final shape of the handle

4. Tillering and Shaping the Handle

Finally, we can put our bow on the tillering stick—really carefully—without overdrawing the bow!

As described in more detail from page 74 on, we tiller the bow until we have achieved the desired draw length and both limbs are bending evenly.

Once we are happy with the profile of the limbs, we give shape to the handle. Again, there are few limits to the design, but we have to keep in mind that the bow should not bend in the handle area. Accordingly, we have to take care that we do not make the handle too thin.

After having outlined and cut out the contours of the handle, we round off the sharp edges with a rasp and file the handle to shape with a rough file.

Using a file, we remove any tool marks left on the surface of the bow and round off the recurves, where necessary.

At last we check the tiller once more. Everything is fine! As the handle does not bend, the shaping of the handle has almost no influence on the tiller. If needed, we would have to do some re-tillering.

After having finished the surface with sandpaper of grit 120, 240 and 500, we remove the sanding dust with a soft brush.

As tung oil accentuates the texture and the natural colors of the wood, we use tung oil as a protective coating for the recurves and the handle. For the rattan limbs, we use an appropriate wax.

Caution: Follow safety instructions and take appropriate precautions! See a more detailed description from page 50 on!

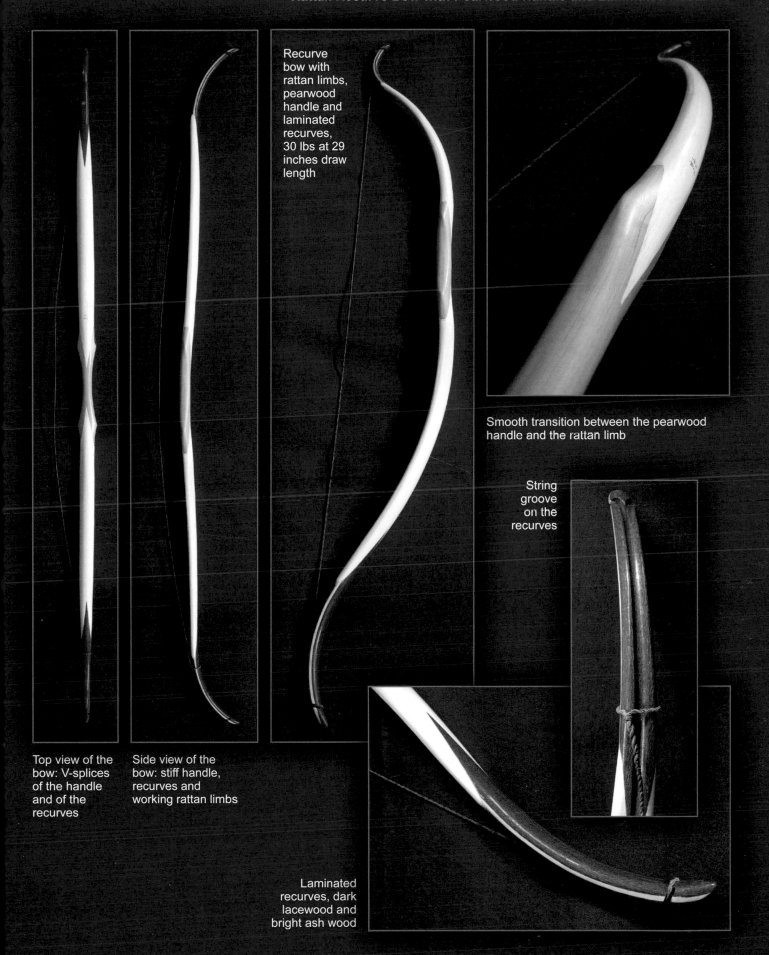

Recurve bow with rattan limbs, pearwood handle and laminated recurves, 30 lbs at 29 inches draw length

Smooth transition between the pearwood handle and the rattan limb

String groove on the recurves

Top view of the bow: V-splices of the handle and of the recurves

Side view of the bow: stiff handle, recurves and working rattan limbs

Laminated recurves, dark lacewood and bright ash wood

APPENDIX

Tools

There are a variety of tools used for bow making. We prefer hand tools, because they are easy to handle without producing too much noise and dust. Some hand tools do not require sharpening and are ideal for bow making (see picture below). Working with a draw knife or a plane is very comfortable and effective, but with these tools it is fundamental that the blade is always kept very sharp, therefore they must be re-sharpened frequently.

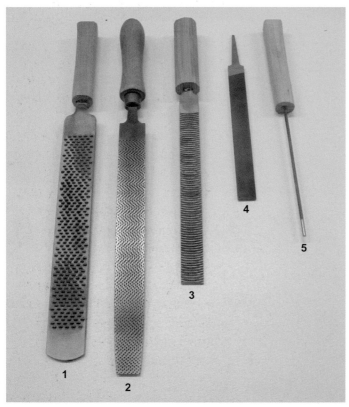

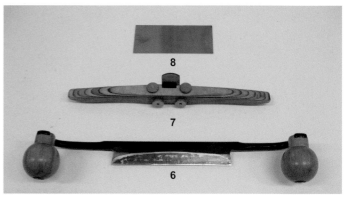

Tools that require sharpening:

6. **Draw knife:** for contouring the bow stave, removes a lot of wood
7. **Scraper plane / spokeshave:** from 1/3 of the intended draw length till completion of the tiller and for removing tool traces, takes off small amounts of wood and leaves an even surface
8. **Scraper:** from 2/3 of the intended draw length and for removing tool traces, takes off small amounts of wood

Tools that do not need sharpening:

1. **Hoof rasp:** very coarse rasp for contouring the bow stave
2. **Medium course rasp:** for the first tillering steps up to 2/3 of the intended draw length
3. **Milled radial file:** for removing rasp traces and for tillering of the last third
4. **Machinist file (cut 0):** for removing residual tool traces after the tillering process
5. **Round file (4 mm):** for making the nock grooves

With these tools, make sure that they are always kept sharpened. Blunt tools involve an increased risk of injury and tear out wood grains.

When sharpening these tools always take the necessary health and safety precautions and follow the sharpening instructions of the manufacturer!

Glossary

BOW:

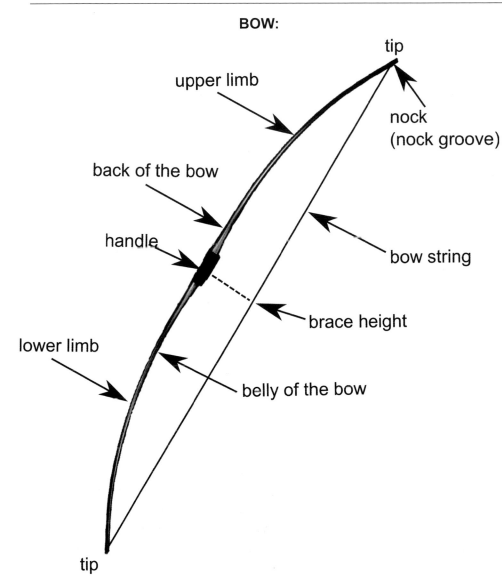

- **Brace height:** measurement for the correct distance of the string from the bow
- **Draw length:** distance between back of the bow and bow string at full draw, measured in inches
- **Draw weight:** force that is needed to pull a bow up to full draw length, measured in pounds (lbs)
- **Finish:** treatment of the surface of the bow with wax or oil
- **Flemish splice string:** bow string made of several strands with a spliced loop (string eye) at one end
- **Handle:** middle part of the bow where the bow is held
- **Inch:** unit of measurement, corresponds to about 25.4 mm
- **Limbs:** the bending parts of a bow, a bow has an upper and a lower limb
- **Nock, nock groove, string groove:** grooves at the end of each limb to hold the bow string
- **Pounds (**abbreviated **lbs):** unit of measurement, corresponds to about 453 grams
- **Stave:** piece of wood with roughly sawn-out shape of the bow
- **String eye:** loop at the end of a bow string for stringing the bow between the nocks
- **Tiller:** bending proportions of the limbs from the side view
- **Tillering:** process of removing wood from a stave to get to the intended bending of the bow
- **Tillering stick:** a board with notches to clamp in the bow stave during the tillering process
- **Tips:** ends of the limbs

- **Annual growth ring:** amount of wood added during a single growth period
- **Back of the bow:** the outward side of the bow turning away from the archer, facing the target (mainly tensile strain)
- **Belly of the bow:** the inward side of the bow facing the archer (mainly compressive strain)
- **Bow stave:** piece of wood with roughly sawn-out shape of the bow

- **Bow string:** string going from one nock to the other that transfers the stored energy to the arrow, twisted of several strands, nowadays usually of synthetic material
- **Bow stringer:** string with leather caps at each end for bracing and unbracing the bow, highly recommended for use during the tillering process and also with the finished bow
- **Bowyer's knot:** knot for Flemish splice bow strings allowing to adjust the length of the bow string

Bow string (Flemish splice)

For the bow string we need two strands of string yarn (for better illustration we are using two different colors here). The length of the strands depends on the length of the bow (bow length plus about 30 cm).
Caution: Follow manufacturer's safety information and recommendations!

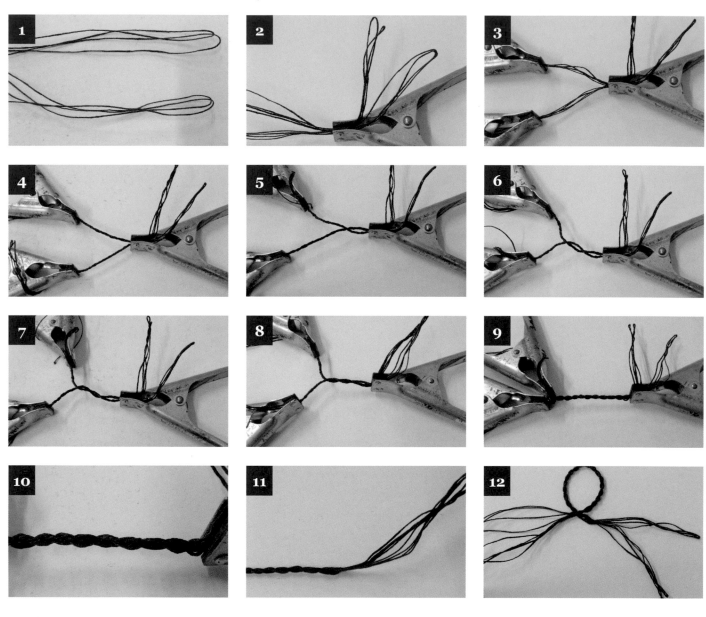

1. The number of threads in one strand depends on the draw weight and on the bowstring material used. For better illustration, we used only four threads for each strand in this example.
2. First we bracket the strands together with a small clamp.

3. On each loose end, we attach another clamp and start twisting each of the two strands in itself to the right.
4 & 5. Then we twist the strands around each other to the left by putting the red strand to the left over the dark strand.
6, 7, 8, 9, 10 & 11 Next, we put the dark one to the left over the red one, and so on in turns, until we have reached a length of about 10 cm.

12. We form a loop (string eye) with the twisted string and adjust the dimension of the loop to the size of the tips.
13 & 14. Now we gather the strands of the same color into pairs of strands (see photo), so that each color, or rather each pair of strands, has one long end and one short end.
15. We twist each pair of strands in itself in a clockwise direction to the right.

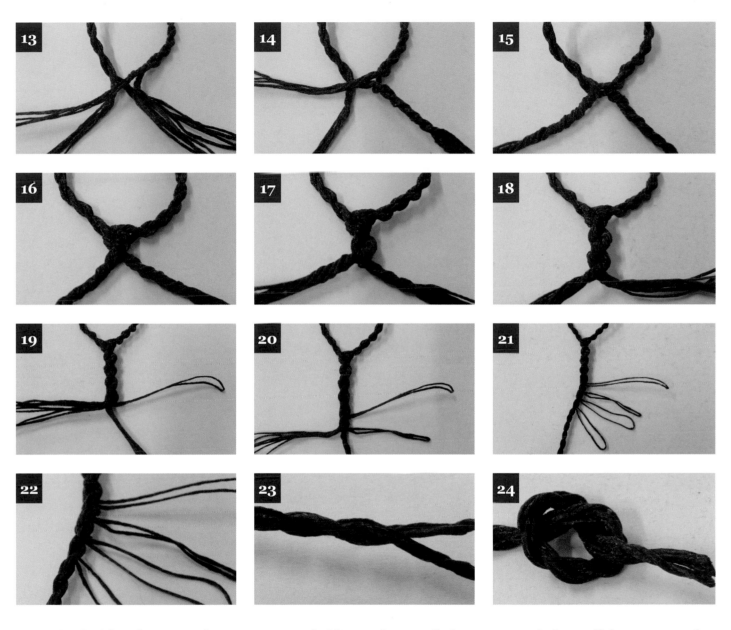

16, 17 & 18. After that, we twist the pairs of strands (twisted in itself to the right) around each other to the left by alternately putting one pair of strands to the left over the other.

19, 20, 21 & 22. After three or four twists, we start to reduce the diameter of the string by pulling out the short ends to the side and stop twisting them with the rest of the strand. After we have pulled out att the short ends one by one, we continue with twisting the long strands (twisted in itself to the right) around each other to the left until we have reached the intended string length. Making sure that we do not damage the bow string, we carefully cut off the short ends sticking out at the sides and singe off the excess end with a cigarette lighter. This forms a small bead at the end of the synthetic thread that prevents the threads from slipping out.

23 & 24. Finally, we secure the end of the bow string with a knot and tighten it securely.

Bowyer's knot

The bowyer's knot tightens under tension and can easily be loosened after release of the strain. With this knot, it is fairly easy to adjust the length of the bow string to the length of the bow.

1. We put the string behind the tip of the limb.
2. We put the loose short end underneath the string and form a loop.
3. Then we put the short end through the loop . . .

4. . . . and lay it over the string, so that we can go through the loop again.
5. We put the short end around the back of the limb, so that both strands lie in front of the limb . . .

6. . . . and pull each strand one by one in the same direction (towards us) until the knot rests tightly in the nock grooves.
7. Finally, we adjust the position of the knot, if necessary, and tighten the knot securely.

Making a bow stringer

The bow stringer should be approximately the same length as the bow stave. Accordingly, we make the nylon cord a little bit longer. We can always shorten it later by adding a few knots. For the caps, we need two strips of leather, about 3 cm in width and 14 cm in length.

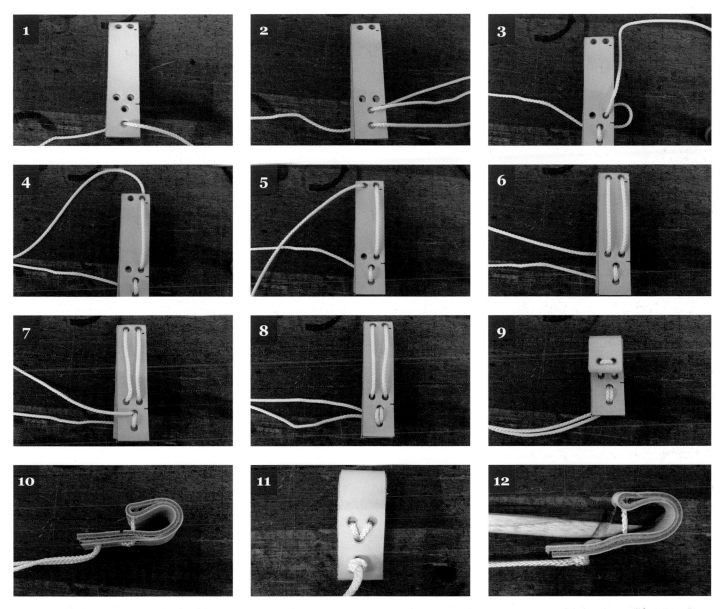

1. Fold the leather strip in the middle. Punch two holes close to the fold, at the open end two holes one above the other, and another two holes.
2. Pull the cord through the bottom hole and then back through the hole above.
3. From bottom up through the right hole at the lower end ...
4. ... and through the right hole at the upper end.
5. Through the left hole of the upper pair back to the top ...
6. ... and over the top side into the left hole at the bottom.
7. Then again from bottom up through the upper single hole ...
8. ... and over the top side back through the bottom single hole.
9. Now tighten the cord, so that the leather strip gets the form of a cap.
10. The bow tips should fit snugly between the caps.
11. On the reverse side, fix the cord with a knot.
12. In the same way, make a cap for the other tip at the other end of the cord.

Library of Congress Control Number: 2013956674

Cover design by John Cheek
Type set in Narkisim, Georgia & Arial

ISBN: 978-0-7643-4546-3
Printed in China

Published by Schiffer Publishing, Ltd.
4880 Lower Valley Road
Atglen, PA 19310
Phone: (610) 593-1777; Fax: (610) 593-2002
E-mail: Info@schifferbooks.com

For our complete selection of fine books on this and related subjects, please visit our website at www.schifferbooks.com. You may also write for a free catalog.

This book may be purchased from the publisher. Please try your bookstore first.

We are always looking for people to write books on new and related subjects. If you have an idea for a book, please contact us at proposals@schifferbooks.com

Schiffer Publishing's titles are available at special discounts for bulk purchases for sales promotions or premiums. Special editions, including personalized covers, corporate imprints, and excerpts can be created in large quantities for special needs. For more information, contact the publisher.

Originally published as Bogenbau mit Manau © 2011 by Kunst-Griff, Linda Schilling & Michael Wlotzka, Berlin, Germany.